T0286951

Cambridge Elements ☰

Elements in Creativity and Imagination
edited by
Anna Abraham
University of Georgia, USA

ITEM RESPONSE THEORY FOR CREATIVITY MEASUREMENT

Nils Myszkowski
Pace University

CAMBRIDGE
UNIVERSITY PRESS

CAMBRIDGE
UNIVERSITY PRESS

Shaftesbury Road, Cambridge CB2 8EA, United Kingdom

One Liberty Plaza, 20th Floor, New York, NY 10006, USA

477 Williamstown Road, Port Melbourne, VIC 3207, Australia

314–321, 3rd Floor, Plot 3, Splendor Forum, Jasola District Centre,
New Delhi – 110025, India

103 Penang Road, #05–06/07, Visioncrest Commercial, Singapore 238467

Cambridge University Press is part of Cambridge University Press & Assessment,
a department of the University of Cambridge.

We share the University's mission to contribute to society through the pursuit of
education, learning and research at the highest international levels of excellence.

www.cambridge.org
Information on this title: www.cambridge.org/9781009475815

DOI: 10.1017/9781009239035

First published 2024

A catalogue record for this publication is available from the British Library.

ISBN 978-1-009-47581-5 Hardback
ISBN 978-1-009-23900-4 Paperback
ISSN 2752-3950 (online)
ISSN 2752-3942 (print)

Item Response Theory for Creativity Measurement

Elements in Creativity and Imagination

DOI: 10.1017/9781009239035
First published online: January 2024

Nils Myszkowski
Pace University

Author for correspondence: Nils Myszkowski, nmyszkowski@pace.edu

Abstract: Item response theory (IRT) represents a key advance in measurement theory. Yet it is largely absent from curricula, textbooks, and popular statistical software and is often introduced through a subset of models. This Element, intended for creativity and innovation researchers, researchers in training, and anyone interested in how individual creativity might be measured, aims to provide: (1) an overview of classical test theory (CTT) and its shortcomings in creativity measurement situations (e.g., fluency scores, consensual assessment technique, etc.); (2) an introduction to IRT and its core concepts, using a broad view of IRT that notably sees CTT models as particular cases of IRT; (3) a practical strategic approach to IRT modeling; (4) example applications of this strategy for creativity research and the associated advantages; and (5) ideas for future work that could advance how IRT could better benefit creativity research as well as connections with other popular frameworks.

Keywords: item response theory, psychometrics, creativity, innovation, test theory, measurement theory, classical test theory, testing

ISBNs: 9781009475815 (HB), 9781009239004 (PB), 9781009239035 (OC)
ISSNs: 2752-3950 (online), 2752-3942 (print)

Contents

1 Introduction

This Element intends to provide researchers and practitioners with an introduction to creativity measurement through the framework of item response theory. While there are several comprehensive books on the vast subject of measurement models and item response theory (for example, De Ayala, 2022), in this Element I specifically focus on providing a concise overview of item response theory and on why, in my opinion, it deserves more attention from creativity researchers.

The rest of this section covers a general discussion of creativity measurement and its challenges. It discusses the (most commonly used) framework of classical test theory, how it is implicitly used through techniques such as sum or average scoring, and its limitations, specifically in the context of creativity measurement. In Section 2, I provide an overview of the framework of item response theory. Item response theory is presented as a general statistical framework for explaining item responses, rather than as a particular set of models. As a consequence, it is presented as a general approach that does not contradict but instead encompasses (or generalizes) classical test theory models. I discuss the different components of item response models, how they are used for measurement (estimation, scoring, item selection, model fit, etc.), and their extensions (multidimensional models, measurement invariance testing, explanatory models, etc.). In Section 3, I provide a short guide to help creativity researchers use item response theory. I discuss how to identify an adequate item distribution, item response, and structural model, and, although this Element does not include a tutorial, I give an overview of the different software that can be used to estimate different models and retrieve information from them. In Section 4, I present different example applications of item response theory in different creativity measurement situations. In Section 5, I discuss what advances one might expect from item response theory modeling that could benefit creativity researchers in the future. I finally close this Element with an encouragement to creativity researchers to consider item response theory in their projects. Supplementary materials are available at https://osf.io/ynt5v/.

Because of the special aim of this Element, a number of topics are only briefly mentioned (e.g., estimation algorithms) or skipped (e.g., Bayesian approaches). Furthermore, although I attempted to make this Element as understandable as possible, it still requires that the reader has some knowledge of key statistical modeling topics. In particular, some prior knowledge of common probability distributions (Gaussian, Bernoulli, Poisson, etc.), (generalized) linear models, test theory, factor analysis, and structural equation modeling would be useful to better grasp all aspects of this Element. In spite of this, I tried to make this Element as self-contained as possible. Illustrating this point, I will start by providing a definition of the measurement of creativity.

1.1 What Does "Measuring Creativity" Mean?

1.1.1 Psychological Measurement

If you aspire to be a mechanic, you cannot resolve to understand cars as mere boxes that take humans from one place to another. While this definition is not incorrect, it would be fatally insufficient. You would not limit your understanding to what cars ultimately achieve but would need to understand *how* they achieve it. Much like being taught how to drive a car but not how it works, psychologists (and others) are often heavily trained in operating tests – how to set the stage, how to prompt answers, how to count points, how to reverse item scores, how to use norms, how to fill forms, and other practical matters – but not so much in how tests function.

Certainly, using a test properly is an important skill that is not easily learned, and making test-using skills central is probably a manifestation of motives beyond psychology – the need to go fast, the fear of mathematics (from students and professors), and the primacy of "being operational." Moreover, psychometric publications (with some notable exceptions) are often hardly readable to nonexperts. Still, a psychological measurement device cannot only be thought of as a behavior-recording machine that – by the magic of sum scores – produces a numeric estimation of a person's attribute. Of course, it seems far-fetched that anyone would present psychological testing in this way. Yet I would argue that it is an accurate – albeit cynical – depiction of how most psychologists view testing. This is not surprising, since this focus on operating tests rather than understanding them is largely propelled by *classical test theory* (CTT), the central framework used to discuss tests in most psychology courses and textbooks (Borsboom, 2006).

Focusing on how to operate tests in a particular way poses a major problem: if we start by how to (conveniently) use a test (e.g., computing sum/average scores to estimate person attributes), then we risk making assumptions that primarily allow us to operate in the way we intend (e.g., stating axioms that support sum/average scoring), without consideration for whether they are realistic, reasonable, or empirically supported. Instead, let us adopt a definition that focuses on the *objective* of testing: *a psychological measurement device – or test – is a device that records and processes a person's behavior(s) in order to provide an accurate statistical estimation of this person's psychological attribute(s).* In general, the behaviors recorded are called *item responses*, and the person's psychological attribute tentatively measured is referred to as the *construct*. As you perhaps guessed from the title of this Element, this definition is closely connected to the definition of *item response theory* (IRT) (see, for example, De Ayala, 2022).

Let us then derive a few key ideas that will later be further developed. First, the probability distribution of the attribute(s) is not yet stated and thus still left open for inquiry or discussion. This is in contrast with CTT (further introduced in Section 1.3), which assumes that the attribute (represented by the true score) follows a particular distribution (a Gaussian distribution) in order to use a number of techniques (e.g., confidence intervals). Second, in this definition, no probability distribution is (yet) specified for item responses (or their errors). This is also in contrast with CTT, which assumes that observed scores (conditional upon the true score) are drawn from a particular distribution (a Gaussian distribution). Third, there may be several attributes measured simultaneously by a set of items. This is also a fundamental departure from CTT, which assumes that a single attribute is measured by a given item. Fourth and finally, the estimation of person attributes requires the estimation and use of a statistical model. This last point is also a fundamental departure from CTT, which treats the estimation of the person attribute as a numeric operation (summing or averaging).

1.1.2 Test Validity and Implications

From our definition of tests, let us define as *test validity* the extent to which a test accurately estimates the psychological attribute(s) of interest – which is relatively in line with the popular definition of validity as "the extent to which a test measures what it purports to measure." Validity (although minimally defined here) is thus the central quality of tests, and it calls for scientific inquiry through the discipline of *psychometrics*. Although psychometrics primarily consists of methods of inquiry, the information that it provides often leads to making modifications to the test to increase its validity (e.g., changing items or changing the scoring procedure) or to make trade-off decisions (e.g., reducing the number of items while retaining sufficient validity).

These definitions of tests and their validity are simple and probably already sound familiar. Nevertheless, they have notable consequences that are not exactly in line with actual research production. First, claims about a person's attribute (say, someone's creativity) can only be substantiated if the test is valid, and therefore evidence of validity is not a detail that can be sidestepped. In other words, using a test and obtaining a score do not constitute proof that measurement has been achieved: this is conditional upon the measurement's validity, which therefore has to be demonstrated.

Second, measurement devices are omnipresent in psychology. They do not have to be called a "test" or a "scale" to be considered as such and thus to require evidence of validity. This is important because, frequently, using an alternative term, such as "task," "rubric," or "checklist," tends to cast a doubt on the amount of psychometric inquiry necessary – after all, it's only a "task," not a "test," right? In the experimental tradition, the word "task" is tradition-ally used, but a task (or a rubric, a checklist, an exam, etc.) is generally used to prompt responses that are then used for the estimation of a person's attribute. Because this absolutely fits our definition, it calls for the same level of psy-chometric inquiry. Psychometric inquiry is equally relevant, whether the test is called a "standardized test," a "cognitive task," a "bio-data checklist," an "exam," or even an "interview rubric." Should the depth of inquiry vary at all, it could depend on the stakes associated with test interpretations (i.e., large-scale assessments used for selection should be more thoroughly examined than a con-sumer survey on preference for ice cream flavors) – more validity is necessary when more is at stake.

Further, this definition of validity is agnostic to whether the test has been published or has gained a large following – in other words, using a test that has been published and/or is popular does not constitute, in and of itself, proof that valid measurement has been achieved. Using extensively used measures can be useful to collect and compile more information regarding a test's valid-ity (provided that such information is produced), but no amount of research on validity constitutes validity. Several popular measures are in fact known to have insufficient evidence of validity – if not evidence of insufficient validity (Borsboom, 2006) – while a new and yet-to-be-studied instrument could have good validity.

1.1.3 Creativity

Let us turn to creativity as the psychological attribute of interest for this Ele-ment. There are many angles that one can use to define creativity. To keep a broad scope, I will not attempt to provide a definition or endorse one in particu-lar. Instead, I will discuss a few alternative conceptualizations of creativity that we will reuse throughout and that you should be familiar with for a better under-standing of the examples, primarily focusing on the creative person, measured directly (e.g., creativity scales) or through their creative products (e.g., con-sensual assessment technique). More comprehensive overviews of creativity measurement can be found (e.g., Qian & Plucker, 2017), but this account should provide sufficiently varied examples that are relatable to researchers in the field.

First, let us note that "creative" is a term that does not only apply to people. It also applies to objects, ideas, and environments, among other things. However, defining the creative product (which can be an idea or an object) is often the basis of other definitions: a creative person can be defined as a person capable of making creative products, a creative environment can be defined as an environment that causes more creative products to be made, and so on and so forth. Consequently, a good starting point is probably the definition of a creative product, which is generally defined as a product that is both original and useful/effective/appropriate (Runco & Jaeger, 2012). Sometimes certain additional features (e.g., stylish, elegant, well-crafted) may be required for a product to be considered creative, depending on the domain (Besemer, 1998).

What follows from this definition is that a creative person is a person who is capable of generating creative products. Depending on the context, we may be interested in a person's creative achievement (what degree of creativity they have demonstrated) or their creative potential (what degree of creativity they are likely to demonstrate). If we are interested in achievement, we often build measurement instruments that probe what a person has done in the past (e.g., if they have composed a song, if they have won awards, etc.). If we are interested in creative potential instead, various measurement paradigms can be used, which typically require people to produce samples of creative work (e.g., we ask a person to invent a story), that imply some measure of the cognitive skills involved in creativity (e.g., divergent thinking) or that imply measures of personality traits or other patterns of behavior frequently seen among creative persons, such as openness or tolerance to ambiguity (for an overview, see Myszkowski, Barbot, & Zenasni, 2022). Finally, it is also possible to assemble measures that rely on these different paradigms into a test battery.

A final important note here is that there is substantial evidence that creativity is at least partly domain specific (Baer, 2012). That is, a person who is creative in one domain (say, generating ideas for scientific inquiry) may not be creative in another domain (say, watercolor painting). This is because, often, being creative requires some level of expertise, which is domain specific, and because being creative in a given domain will often require specific resources (e.g., some creative domains may require more analytical thinking than others).

1.2 An Overview of Measurement Issues in Creativity

From the little we have discussed regarding creativity, we can see how complex the issue of creativity measurement can be. Let us try to list a few of the challenges that researchers and practitioners face when attempting to measure creativity, in the hope that the measurement framework discussed here may provide some solutions.

1.2.1 Multidimensional Constructs

The measurement of creativity commonly raises issues of multidimensionality, for several reasons. First, the consensual definition of creativity as a combination of originality and usefulness (and in some cases, more features) is itself multidimensional. Second, as previously discussed, creativity is partly domain specific, which implies that it takes multiple forms. Another layer of multidimensionality is added by the fact that creativity can be thought of as a result of several other attributes (e.g., divergent thinking, integrative thinking), and the measurement of these attributes may be used in the measurement of creativity. Finally, I set aside the issue of involving raters in some creativity measurement paradigms (I discuss the issue of shared method/nuisance factors later), but dependencies induced by the use of raters can also be seen as a case of multidimensionality. Overall, in creativity psychology, truly unidimensional measures tend to be exceptions.

1.2.2 Varied Item Distributions

When a person responds to an item, it yields an observation: the item score. Let us do a quick thought experiment and imagine having a person respond to a given item several times. We can imagine that we would not necessarily observe the same response every time. As a consequence, in test theory, item responses are seen as random variables. To represent random variables, we generally use a probability distribution model – that is, we identify a probability distribution that we think represents or mimics the random process at play when a person responds. This decision is often referred to as making a *distributional assumption* for the item responses. As we will see later, the Gaussian distribution serves as distributional assumption in classical test theory – which allows certain conveniences (notably using sum/average scores). What is the problem with making such an assumption in creativity measurement? Gaussian distributions – further discussed in Section 1.3.6 – are continuous symmetrical distributions, and their draws are real numbers between $-\infty$ and $+\infty$. Yet many measurement paradigms in creativity research do not yield item scores that are continuous, unbounded, or symmetrical. For example, a divergent thinking task will (notably) generate count data (the number of ideas produced), which are integer (and thus discrete) with a lower bound of 0. As another example, a remote associates test item will generate only two possible observations (pass–fail). As a third example, creative products will in general be rated on an ordinal scale, thus generating discrete data with a lower and an upper bound. In addition to these examples, other measurement tools are yet to be explored in creativity measurement that would disqualify Gaussian item distributional assumptions: for example, a set of ratings of creative products could well generate continuous bounded responses if the rater used a slider scale. Finally, one could encounter situations where multiple item response formats are used in one instrument (e.g., in a test battery situation).

As we can see from these examples, the Gaussian distribution, although it can, in some cases, serve as sufficient approximation, is hardly ideal. We can also see from the variety of these examples that different distributional assumptions may be more appropriate, depending on the type of item (binary, ordinal, count, etc.).

1.2.3 Nuisance Factors and Local Dependencies

According to reflective measurement theory, the measurement of psychological constructs is obtained through inferring from their manifestations (i.e., the item responses). Consequently, such an inference is facilitated if the causal relation between the construct and the item is strong and if the item is not caused by substantial extraneous factors. Creativity is so domain-specific that it is difficult to build items that measure it (or even its components) "purely." Consider, for example, a divergent thinking task where examinees have to produce as many instances of uses of a knife as possible. It can be seen that, for a given divergent thinking level, a person with more experience in certain domains (e.g., cooking) would provide more ideas than a person with less experience in these domains (Myszkowski & Storme, 2021). Thus responses to this item would not be only related to divergent thinking but also to other factors (e.g., some domain-specific knowledge). In addition to the existence of these factors, in creativity research, their confounding effects are often unplanned, unknown, and variable from item to item.

Additionally, even within a micro-domain, creativity involves multiple cognitive abilities and skills, and some of them may be disproportionately captured through the measurement procedure (Silvia, Beaty, & Nusbaum, 2013). For example, when using tests of divergent thinking where individuals have to write many ideas in a limited time, the number of ideas may be related to verbal skills that facilitate their expression of their ideas (i.e., writing speed) but that play a smaller role in the ability to generate ideas.

Finally, similar issues may occur from rater effects. Indeed, if several judges are asked to rate the creativity of stimuli – a classic measurement paradigm in creativity (Amabile, 1982) – then the ratings themselves are not solely explained by the creativity of the creator – they may be, at least partly, explained by characteristics of the rater (e.g., expertise, severity).

In general, these factors, which are measured along with the construct of interest – and thus undesirable – are referred to as *nuisance factors* or *method variance factors*. We could also think of them as sources of violations of *conditional independence*, meaning that item responses are related to each other over and above their relations with the construct(s). One may attempt to reduce the impact of nuisance factors by changing the measurement paradigm experimentally. For example, for domain specificity in a divergent thinking task, we can try to make the object used as a prompt as domain-free as possible (asking for uses of a knife rather than uses of a tuning fork, for example). To control experimentally for writing speed, we could imagine that the responses are spoken rather than written. To control for rater effects experimentally, we could make rating instructions very coded and specific. Nevertheless, these attempts to mitigate the effect of nuisance factors may be impossible, inefficient, or even counterproductive. For example, by replacing *writing* ideas with *saying* ideas, we might actually replace the nuisance factor of writing speed with that of oral communication skills and/or social (dis)inhibition, perhaps introducing more severe threats to test validity. Likewise, making rating instructions too specific and multiplying them could lead to measuring a narrowed version of the construct of creativity. Because of these challenges, a psychometric framework that allows the detection of and control for nuisance factors statistically is desirable.

1.2.4 Heterogeneous Populations

The multidimensionality of creativity often implies that we cannot be certain that a measurement device functions similarly for all persons measured. In the previous example of divergent thinking tasks, generating ideas for using an object might be influenced by a person's age (because they could have more knowledge and perhaps have used the object more). As a consequence, a test measuring divergent thinking with these items may become easier with age. To ensure validity, we may want to ensure that the measurement has constant properties for all persons measured and at all times. This property is generally referred to as *measurement invariance*. It is preferable to use a measurement framework that allows us to detect and quantify a lack of measurement invariance as well as to control for it.

Moreover, in creativity research, the population may be heterogeneous without a clear definition of the variables that cause its heterogeneity. For example, when studying creativity, we may sample from a population that contains individuals who are completely naïve, who are experts or professionals in the domain measured, who are experts in connected domains, who are not experts but are deeply interested in the domain or related topics, and so on. This idea of different classes of creative ability has been extensively discussed in creativity research, notably with the theory of the four Cs of creativity (Kaufman & Beghetto, 2009). A framework capable of measuring heterogeneous populations and of disentangling classes of individuals not identified a priori is thus particularly relevant in creativity research.

1.3 Classical Test Theory as the Typical Toolkit

In this section, I will summarize the framework and practice of classical test theory. Afterwards I will discuss how it is typically implemented in research and its shortcomings when it comes to creativity measurement.

1.3.1 The "True" Score

Classical test theory (CTT) is certainly the most popular psychological measurement framework. It describes how observed scores result from the sum of a "true score" component and a random error component (for this reason, CTT is also called true score theory). This framework is typically summarized with the following equation, where x represents a person's observed score at a given item, t represents a person's "true score," and e represents a random (Gaussian) error:

$$x = t + e.$$

There are variations of this equation, which we will discuss later. However, we can first note that, so far, there is no psychological attribute in this definition but a "true score" instead. While the equation just presented may appear very convincing and appealing due to its tautological nature – after all, an observed score will always be equal to its expectation plus an error – it already presents an important flaw: Where is the psychological attribute that we wanted to estimate? Did we really want to estimate a score – however true it may be – in the first place?

Certainly, our goal might be to estimate the "true score" in order to use it as a proxy for the psychological attribute. The true score shares some common characteristics with a psychological attribute in that it is an unobserved variable that depends on the person and has an effect on observed scores. Still, a key distinction between the true score and a psychological construct is that the true score depends not only on the person but also on the instrument – as the name "score" suggests. For example, a true score for a set of pass–fail items in a remote associate test is comprised between 0 (fail) and 1 (pass), while a true score on a 5-point ordinal scale for ratings of creative stories is comprised between 1 and 5. Further, a difficult test will have lower true scores than an easy test – all else being equal and with higher scores indicating success. This entanglement between person and test characteristics, which leads to person estimates being dependent on the test and test/item estimates being dependent on the person measured, is central to a number of shortcomings that we will later discuss.

At this stage, the "true score" t is essentially a hyperbolic term for the expectation of the observed score (i.e., $E(x)$). Yet if we admit that we want to use this expectation as a proxy for the construct, then CTT appears practical, because then the mean of observed scores across items for a given person provides us with an estimate of the true score (although this is not true of all CTT variations, as we will see). Further, the ratio between the variance of t and the variance of x can be used as an estimate of "how similar the true score is to the observed scores" – in other words as a measure of reliability – from which standard errors of measurement can be derived.

Classical test theory being (apparently) easy to understand, true (because it is tautologically rather than statistically presented), and easy to operate without statistical estimation, it is of course very appealing. To better understand it, we need to get to the details of its variations, which I will now describe, from the most constrained model to the least constrained. For readers interested in more extensive descriptions and proofs of the implications, see Lord and Novick (2008).

1.3.2 The Parallel CTT Model

The CTT model for *parallel* items assumes that items are perfectly interchangeable within a test. In other words, for a person i and an item j, the observed score x_{ij} is given by a true score t_i that, for a given test, only depends on the person. The random component e_{ij} is drawn from a Gaussian distribution of mean 0 and variance σ^2. The σ^2 distributional parameter does not depend on the item (or the person). We can write:

$$x_{ij} = t_i + e_{ij},$$
$$e_{ij} \sim N(0, \sigma^2).$$

In general, CTT revolves around the true score, not around person characteristics. Still, in practice, estimations of the true score are used as person estimates. For consistency with how we will express IRT models throughout, let us reformulate CTT models more explicitly, using a latent person attribute instead of the true score.

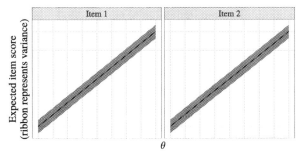

Figure 1 Example item response functions of the parallel CTT model

In the parallel model, scores are assumed to be random draws from a Gaussian distribution of location (mean) μ_i and of fixed scale (variance) σ^2. The distribution parameter μ_i is defined for this model as equal to a person i's latent attribute θ_i. To note, in Gaussian distributions, the expectation $E(x)$ is equal to the location/mean distributional parameter μ. To sum up, we have:

$$\mu_i = E(x_i) = \theta_i,$$
$$x_{ij} \sim \mathcal{N}(\mu_i, \sigma^2).$$

The function that gives an expected item score $E(x_{ij})$ as a function of a latent attribute θ_i is generally referred to in IRT as the *item response function*. In the parallel model, since the expected item response is equal to θ_i, the item response function is the *identity function* $(f(x) = x)$, which is a particular case of a linear function (with slope 1 and intercept 0). For illustration, I show the example of expected scores for two parallel items (i.e., their item response functions) in Figure 1.

For parallel items, the mean of a person's item scores directly provides a (maximum likelihood) estimate of the person location. Measurement can thus, under this model, be achieved without requiring statistical estimation. Also, since all items have the same variance, reliability only depends on test length (how many items there are), not on which items are used. According to this model, we can therefore also predict the reliability of an instrument given its length for a given test (through the Spearman–Brown reliability prophecy formula).

1.3.3 The Tau-Equivalent CTT Model

In practice, when taking tests, individuals fluctuate in (notably) attention and fatigue (see, for example, Myszkowski, Storme, Kubiak, et al., 2022), so measurement errors can rarely be assumed to have the same magnitude across items. To account for this, the CTT model for *tau-equivalent* items relaxes the assumption that error variances are the same across items:

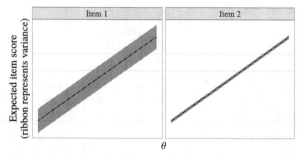

Figure 2 Example item response functions of the tau-equivalent CTT model

$$x_{ij} = t_i + e_{ij},$$
$$e_{ij} \sim N(0, \sigma_j^2).$$

Like the parallel model, this model can be reformulated in a probabilistic manner:

$$\mu_i = E(x_i) = \theta_i,$$
$$x_{ij} \sim N(\mu_i, \sigma_j^2).$$

For illustration, I show the example of expected scores for two tau-equivalent items (i.e., their item response functions) in Figure 2. It can be seen that the item response functions are the same (both the identity function), while the items differ in their error variances (represented by the width of the ribbon).

The parallel model is a particular case of the tau-equivalent model (Graham, 2006), with σ_j^2 constrained equal across all items. Relaxing this assumption implies that some items may produce larger errors than others. Therefore, reliability can no longer be predicted as a function of test length only. Further, if the test is, for example, split in half randomly, the two halves are not guaranteed to have equal reliability. However, like the parallel model, a person's average score across items provides an estimate of θ_i, which allows measurement without statistical model estimation.

1.3.4 The Essentially Tau-Equivalent CTT Model

Within a test, items often vary in difficulty – or, for self-report scales, in the difficulty of endorsing a statement. Thus the true score may change according to the location of an item on a difficulty continuum. The CTT model for *essentially tau-equivalent* items accommodates this by not assuming the same true score across items. It assumes instead that the true score is the sum of a person's true score (which, for convenience with our IRT notation, we will directly note

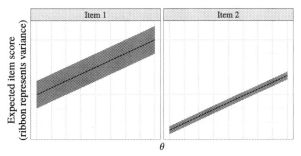

Figure 3 Example item response functions of the essentially tau-equivalent CTT model

as θ_i) and an item location parameter b_j, which represents item j's location (higher values indicate lower difficulty):

$$x_{ij} = t_{ij} + e_{ij},$$
$$t_{ij} = \theta_i + b_j,$$
$$e_{ij} \sim \mathcal{N}(0, \sigma_j^2).$$

Like before, we may express it as:

$$\mu_{ij} = E(x_{ij}) = \theta_i + b_j,$$
$$x_{ij} \sim \mathcal{N}(\mu_{ij}, \sigma_j^2).$$

For illustration, I show the example of expected scores for two essentially tau-equivalent items (i.e., their item response functions) in Figure 3. It can be seen that the items now differ in their error variances and in their difficulty parameters (represented by the varying intercept of the lines).

In the essentially tau-equivalent model, the response function is no longer the identity function but a *linear function* (i.e., an affine function). Thus the person's characteristic θ_i cannot be estimated by simply averaging observed scores. However, given a test, the order of person attributes is (expected to be) preserved when using average/sum scores. In other words, sum/average scores can be used to compare person locations, provided that the same items are used. We will later come back to this property, but we can note that, in the IRT tradition, this feature is referred to as invariant item ordering. In CTT, the parallel, tau-equivalent, and essentially tau-equivalent models all imply invariant item ordering. As a side note, it can be seen that the tau-equivalent model is a particular case of the essentially tau-equivalent model (Graham, 2006), with b_j fixed to 0 across all items. Because the parallel model is a particular case of the tau-equivalent model, it is also a particular case of the essentially tau-equivalent model.

1.3.5 The Congeneric CTT Model

The congeneric model relaxes an additional assumption, as it allows the strength (and direction) of the relation between the attribute and the item response to differ across items. It does so by introducing an additional item parameter, a_j. In reference to linear models, this parameter can be referred to as a *slope*, but in the factor analysis tradition it is often called a *loading*. In the IRT tradition it is often referred to as a *discrimination parameter*, because larger (positive or negative) values imply that item scores are more sensitive to between-person variability.

$$x_{ij} = t_{ij} + e_{ij},$$
$$t_{ij} = a_j\theta_i + b_j,$$
$$e_{ij} \sim \mathcal{N}(0, \sigma_j^2).$$

Again, we can alternatively write this model as:

$$\mu_{ij} = E(x_{ij}) = a_j\theta_i + b_j,$$
$$x_{ij} \sim \mathcal{N}(\mu_{ij}, \sigma_j^2).$$

The congeneric model notably underlies (linear) factor analysis models. For illustration, I show the example of expected scores for two congeneric items in Figure 4. It can be seen that the items now differ in their error variances (represented by the width of the ribbon), in their location (represented by the varying intercept of the lines), and in their discrimination (represented by the varying slopes). Contrary to the previously presented CTT models, the item response functions of the items intersect. Consequently, the order across persons given a test is not preserved by sum/average scores. Thus this model does not support sum/average scores for person measurement (see McNeish & Wolf, 2020). The essentially tau-equivalent model is a particular case of the congeneric model (Graham, 2006) with a_j constrained to 1 across all items. Because

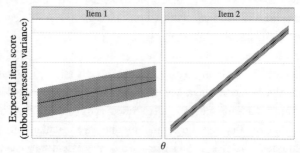

Figure 4 Example item response functions of the congeneric CTT model

the tau-equivalent and parallel models are particular cases of the essentially tau-equivalent model, they are also particular cases of the congeneric model.

1.3.6 Structural and Distributional Assumptions of CTT Models

For a clearer understanding of the following, let us consider again the most general formulation of the CTT model, which is the congeneric model:

$$\mu_{ij} = E(x_{ij}) = a_j\theta_i + b_j,$$
$$x_{ij} \sim N(\mu_{ij}, \sigma_j^2).$$

The first part of this response model is generally referred to as the *structural assumption* of the model. In measurement (like in statistical modeling in general), a structural assumption specifies relations between different variables (here expected item scores and item/person characteristics).

For all CTT models, which can all be expressed as cases of the congeneric model, the relation between the latent person characteristic θ_i and the expected item response is assumed to be *linear* (the identity function, used for the parallel and tau-equivalent models, is a particular case of a linear function). Thus all CTT models use linear item response functions. We will refer to this later as the *linearity assumption*, and we will see that IRT does not present this limitation.

The second part of this formulation is generally referred to as the *distributional assumption* of the model. For all CTT models, the response x_{ij} (conditional upon the true score t_{ij}) is assumed to come from a Gaussian distribution. Gaussian (or normal) distributions have two distributional parameters: a location (or mean) parameter μ and a scale (or variance) parameter σ^2. Figure 5 illustrates how the location and scale parameters modify the Gaussian distribution. We can see that higher μ values move the distribution to the right (i.e., higher observations are more probable), while higher σ^2 values indicate that observations are scattered further from the mean. In CTT models, the location μ_{ij} is equal to the expected item score and thus given by the response model directly. The scale parameter of the Gaussian distribution σ_j^2 is said to be constant, in that it is fixed across all persons for a given item – we refer to this assumption as the *homoscedasticity assumption*. It implies that, for a given item, the same amount of error is expected from every person measured. In other words, in CTT, it is assumed that an item (and consequently an entire test) is equally reliable for all persons measured.

We will later discuss how an important advantage of IRT is that it can make other distributional assumptions (e.g., Poisson, binomial, multinomial, gamma), which often offer a more accurate representation of measurement paradigms. We will also see that many of these distributions do not assume

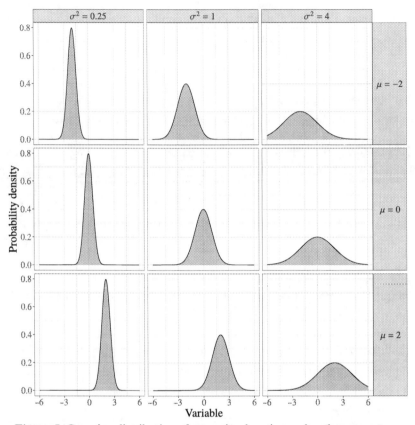

Figure 5 Gaussian distributions for varying location and scale parameters
Note: The Gaussian distribution of location $\mu = 0$ and scale $\sigma^2 = 1$, represented in the middle of this figure, is known as the standard normal (or z) distribution.

variance to be homogeneous and often provide more reasonable assumptions regarding item score variances.

1.3.7 Consequences of CTT for Psychometric Practice

Classical test theory models certainly offer practicalities. Notably, the parallel and tau-equivalent models support sum or average scores as estimators of the true score, thus providing person estimates arithmetically, without requiring statistical estimation. A corollary is that when a person is measured through some sum or average scoring, the implicit assumption (although rarely tested or even discussed) is typically that the parallel or tau-equivalent CTT model is true (see Graham, 2006; McNeish & Wolf, 2020).

Another common practice is to provide some estimate of measurement accuracy through Cronbach's α (which is used as an estimate of reliability and/or transformed into a standard error of measurement or confidence intervals). As has been heavily discussed in psychometrics, Cronbach's α assumes a CTT tau-equivalent model, which implies that when Cronbach's α is reported, one implicitly assumes a CTT tau-equivalent to be true – again, this is not frequently tested (Graham, 2006). When this assumption is violated, estimates of reliability (as well as standard errors of measurement and score confidence intervals, if computed from it) may be inaccurate.

Although these points may seem trivial, I invite you to consider altogether how many measurement instruments use sum (or average) scores for person measurement. Next, consider how many of these had supporting evidence either that (1) a tau-equivalent or parallel CTT model was empirically supported and not outperformed by, for example, a congeneric model, or that (2) sum or average scores were perfectly (or nearly enough) correlated with person estimates from a model that was supported empirically.

1.3.8 Unidimensionality and Factor Analysis

We will later discuss dimensionality extensively, but let us note that all the CTT models discussed so far are *unidimensional*. This means that a single person characteristic θ_i is assumed to cause the item scores, as can be seen from the structural assumption of all CTT models previously discussed.

What about factor analysis? Certainly, there are some techniques that are used along with CTT practices that can accommodate multidimensional situations. More specifically, linear (i.e., traditional) factor analysis (exploratory and confirmatory) allows multiple person latent variables (i.e., multidimensional models). However, these techniques are, in practice, mostly used temporarily, in order to investigate or verify the structural validity of instruments, and then set aside and not used for person measurement. It is important to remember that achieving measurement is about estimating the person's characteristic – no matter what additional analyses are done "on the side." When one computes a sum or average score to estimate a person's characteristic, they assume the model that supports such estimation, which is the (unidimensional) parallel (or tau-equivalent) CTT model (McNeish & Wolf, 2020). Thus while psychometric investigation may invite multidimensional models, actual measurement practice generally implies unidimensionality.

In addition to this, factor analysis corresponds to the definition and characteristics of IRT – not CTT. Consider, for example, that Novick (1966, pp. 1–2) defines CTT as the "theory which postulates the existence of a true score, that error scores are uncorrelated with each other and with true scores and that observed, true and error scores are linearly related." Factor analysis does not

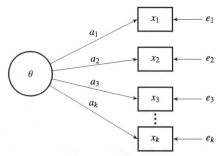

Figure 6 Typical representation of the congeneric model (for *k* items) as a
path diagram in the factor analytic tradition
Note: Intercepts (including item location parameters) are usually not
estimated for these models and thus not represented on the diagram (triangles
are used to represent them if useful).

meet this definition so well: it does not require us to assume a true score, it
can be used to study whether errors are correlated or not (more on this point
later), and it can even be nonlinear. Now, let us consider that IRT is generally
defined as a framework that provides testable models that connect person-latent
variables with the item scores (De Ayala, 2022) and that the "ultimate defining
characteristic of IRT" (van der Linden, 2016, p. 8) is the separation of person
characteristics and item characteristics. Factor analysis actually meets that definition quite well: it does provide testable models that connect person-latent
variables with item responses, and person characteristics (with latent variables) and item characteristics (with item loadings and intercepts, generally)
are indeed separable in factor analysis. Thus I would argue that factor analysis
should be regarded as an application of IRT, not as an application of CTT. In
Figure 6, I show how the congeneric CTT model is typically represented in the
factor analysis tradition.

1.3.9 Reflective Measurement and Local Independence

In CTT, observed scores (i.e., item responses) are explained by the "true score,"
which is used as a proxy for the psychological construct. In other words, CTT is
built around the idea that an unobserved attribute serves as explanation for the
item scores. Alternatively, we could say that item scores are manifestations of
– or caused by – person attributes. For example, we assume that high divergent
thinking causes a participant to generate many original and useful ideas. This
representation of measurement, which states that latent attributes are causes of
observed item responses, is generally referred to as the *reflective measurement*

framework – or as the *Causal Theory of Measurement (CTM)* – and is common to CTT and IRT.

Directly related to this is the assumption of CTT that the item scores are unrelated to one another once we account for them being caused by the latent attribute (through the true score in CTT) (Novick, 1966). This assumption is generally referred to as the assumption of *local independence* or *conditional independence*. Using the previous example, all observed relations between scores in a set of divergent thinking items are assumed to be *solely* explained by them being caused by the same construct (divergent thinking ability). While it is an assumption of both CTT and IRT, IRT allows the study of and accounting for violations of local independence. Such violations are generally referred to as *local dependencies* (LD) in IRT (and as correlated residuals in factor analysis). Reflective measurement and local independence go hand in hand: the explanation for the relations between items is a (set of) latent attribute(s) (reflective measurement) and the latent attribute(s) only (local independence). In the last section of this Element, we discuss hybrids of reflective/locally independent measurement and methods for nonreflective and locally dependent methods.

1.4 The Shortcomings of Classical Test Theory for Creativity Measurement

We have previously discussed the main challenges of creativity measurement and the various assumptions of CTT models. Let us now consider the insufficiency of CTT in the context of creativity measurement.

1.4.1 A Source of Conceptual Confusion

As we noted, the parallel and the tau-equivalent models – which are assumed by sum/average scoring – equate the latent attribute being measured with the expected item score. This is a source of confusion in the field of psychology in general (Borsboom, 2006; Borsboom & Mellenbergh, 2002) and in creativity psychology as well. Because psychological attributes and expected item score are axiomatically equated, and since average (or sum) scores are used to approximate the person attribute, it is tempting to assign features observed for average and sum scores to the attribute measured – in other words, to mistake observed score characteristics for attribute characteristics.

Let us illustrate these issues with a thought experiment. Consider a single personality item, "Do you consider yourself to have a creative personality?" People are invited to respond either yes or no. Because the scores are binary, would you conclude that creative personality is binary (i.e., that a person is either creative or uncreative, with nothing in between)? No, and you would be right. Sure, so what if we had 10 items? The distribution of average scores would not be binary anymore. But has the distribution of creativity changed? Of course not: it is the measurement device that has changed.

Examples of this confusion are commonplace in psychology in general, creativity psychology included. Batey (2012), for example, discusses how "trait creativity" differs from creativity achievement due to the scores observed following different distributions – "trait" measures yield approximately normally distributed scores, while "achievement" measures yield Poisson-distributed scores. Divergent thinking is, in the same paper, provided as an example of "trait creativity" (i.e., normally distributed creativity), yet a fluency score on a divergent thinking task is in fact better approximated by a model assuming Poisson-distributed scores (Myszkowski & Storme, 2021). So does divergent thinking, when measured through fluency, become part of the achievement creativity kind as a consequence? While it is possible that the two constructs have different distributions (and while the question remains largely unstudied), the different distributions of observed scores are probably a cause of the measurement apparatus, not of the underlying psychological attribute.

This is only one example (in a paper that in spite of this makes a lot of interesting points) of how equating scores with psychological attributes – which is often referred to as the *Platonic interpretation of the true score* (Lord & Novick, 2008) – results in confusion: Are we talking about scores or constructs? The implications of this fallacy in creativity psychology still have to be extensively reviewed (for an introduction to this problem, see Borsboom & Mellenbergh, 2002; Lumsden, 1976). In any case, a framework that does not invite such misinterpretations is preferable.

1.4.2 Issues That Pertain to Structural Complexity and Local Dependencies

We have noted that the structure of creativity measures can be quite complex for several reasons. Notably, one often requires raters to judge products. In creativity psychology, we are well aware that judges have an effect on the item scores (Kaufman, Baer, & Cole, 2009; Myszkowski & Storme, 2019; Storme, Myszkowski, Çelik, et al., 2014). Thus scores are not only caused by a person's creativity but also by rater characteristics. Rater effects could also be considered as local dependencies, but in any case, this situation leads to violations of the assumptions of CTT models.

As we noted, multidimensionality and/or local dependencies often come from measurement paradigms where both general and specific attributes are involved – they are often referred to as testlets, specific factors, or shared method variance factors, depending on the context. For example, general creativity and some domain- or prompt-specific creativity factor may simultaneously cause responses to a creativity task. We could imagine a situation where examinees, for a divergent thinking measure, have to produce many original ideas in different tasks, which use different types of prompts (e.g., alternate uses vs. imaginary animal names). We would want to represent this situation by stating that there are in fact local dependencies, because there may be some relations, over and beyond divergent thinking (the general factor), between the item scores.

1.4.3 Issues That Pertain to Item Distributions

Items come in many shapes when it comes to creativity measurement, making the assumption that their errors follow a (homoscedastic) Gaussian distribution often questionable. Before we move on, let us be reminded of important features that characterize the normal distribution. First, the normal distribution is continuous, meaning that it produces an infinite number of possible values between any two values. Second, the normal distribution is unimodal and symmetric around the center of the distribution, which is simultaneously the mean, the median, and the mode of the distribution. Finally, it is unbounded, meaning that it has no upper or lower bound. Because it is both continuous and unbounded, its support (the set of observable realizations) is $\mathbb{R}$ (i.e., $]-\infty, +\infty[$).

In contrast, many measures used in creativity psychology produce scores that are discrete and/or bounded. In creativity, we often deal with binary (e.g, remote associates test item responses, biodata checklists) or polytomous (e.g., consensual assessment technique ratings, self-report personality measures) responses. Further, item responses may be counts (e.g., divergent thinking fluency scores), which are discrete with a lower bound. Some other measures may also be continuous but bounded – for example, the relative (in)frequency of ideas in divergent thinking tasks is typically bounded (between 0 and 1).

Further, there are some cases in which the distributions may not be assumed to be symmetric. For example, divergent thinking fluency scores are often positively skewed and not symmetric (Forthmann, Paek, Dumas, et al., 2020). In fact, sometimes researchers resort to over-instructing raters – which may impact construct validity – in order to obtain ratings that are somewhat symmetric (e.g., instructions like "aim to give this proportion of 1s, this proportion of 2s, etc.") (Myszkowski & Storme, 2019).

In addition, it is often unreasonable to assume that the error distributions are homoscedastic. Take the example of a remote associates test item of average difficulty (scored 0 for fail and 1 for pass). Person A has a low ability, person B an average ability, and person C a high ability. Because persons A and C have respectively a low and a high ability, their probability of succeeding is close to 0 and 1, respectively. Thus their actual score is predicted with precision: person A will quite probably score 0 and person C 1. In contrast, because person B has an average ability, their probability of succeeding should be closer to 0.5, and consequently we cannot predict their score with great certainty. You would thus expect error variance to vary by person for a given item (i.e., heteroscedasticity).

To sum up, although they may be sufficiently accurate in some cases, the distributional assumptions of CTT models are often unrealistic in the context of creativity measurement, calling for more flexibility.

1.4.4 Issues That Pertain to Linearity

Classical test theory assumes that the relation between the latent attribute and the item response is linear. This is problematic for many creativity measures. Notably, linear models will tend to make predictions that go beyond the bounds of the item responses. In Figure 7, I show how this poses issues: for binary responses, scores beyond 0 and 1 are predicted; in count responses, negative counts are predicted; for polytomous responses, scores beyond the lowest and highest options are expected.

In addition, bounds often impose a particular shape on the item response function – this is often referred to as a *floor* (for lower bounds) or a *ceiling* (for upper bounds) effect. As the item response approaches the bounds, it tends to be constrained by the bound and thus changes less as a function of a latent attribute. In other words, as the item response approaches the bounds, the item response function becomes more horizontal (the horizontal line that it tends to is referred to as an *asymptote*). For example, for count items, the presence of a lower bound of 0 for the item response (the vertical axis) calls for a response function with a lower asymptote (later, we will see that a frequent choice for such a function is the exponential function). Items with both a lower and an upper bound will call for response functions with both a lower and an upper asymptote (later, we will see that a frequent choice is the logistic function).

1.4.5 Issues That Pertain to the Tautological Nature of CTT

Measuring psychological attributes is a strong and important claim, and it should be supported empirically. Unfortunately, although CTT variations can be described as testable models, the way that CTT is formulated – as a tautology (Lord & Novick, 2008) – encourages researchers to adopt an operationalist view of measurement that bypasses empirical and conceptual inquiry regarding the assumed model (Borsboom, 2006).

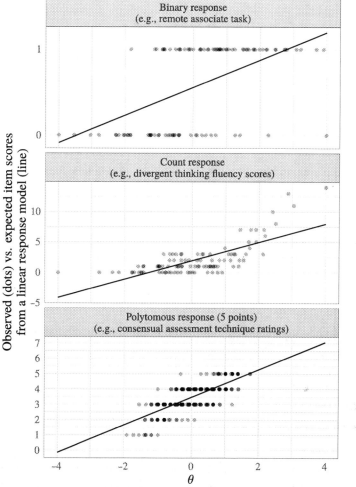

Figure 7 Illustration of the problems of using linear models to predict binary, count, and polytomous responses

In other words, CTT provides an alibi to assume – through the use of sum scores and Cronbach's α (Borsboom, 2006; McNeish & Wolf, 2020) – a psychometric model without a discussion of whether accurate measurement is achieved. Frequently, we are tempted to state "we measured creativity" (or any other construct) without showing any empirical proof that, for example, a single attribute is the most probable cause for the item scores (i.e., without showing that a unidimensional model is a good predictor of the item scores or their relations) – note that Cronbach's α assumes unidimensionality but is not a measure of it (Zinbarg, Yovel, Revelle, et al., 2006). Therefore CTT provides a bypass for rather than a solution to the problem of psychological measurement.

Adopting a framework that formulates how an instrument functions and tests such a formulation statistically before estimating person attributes simply represents a more scientific approach.

1.4.6 Impracticalities

While we have discussed CTT as practical due to the ease of average scoring, it is not practical for many situations and frequently requires a number of additional procedures.

First, because CTT models are linear and assume homogeneous errors, they assume that, for a given item as well as for a given test, all individuals are measured with equal reliability. This assumption is a bit counterintuitive: it appears logical that, for example, if an item (or a test) is very easy, it will more reliably measure the person's attribute if they have a low level of that attribute. For example, if we build an item that asks for original ways to solve a high school level geometry problem, a high school student would be more reliably measured than a toddler – for whom the item would be too difficult – or a PhD student in mathematics – for whom the item would be too easy. Thus we may expect from a measurement framework that it considers that different persons may be measured with different levels of reliability, because it makes sense conceptually to expect that.

Second, the assumption of homoscedasticity implies that we can identify items with smaller errors for all persons but not items that would reduce measurement error for a person specifically. In general, we want to assemble tests that are particularly appropriate for a person's anticipated level.

Another problem of CTT practice is that with sum or average scoring, a person's location in relation to the population of interest is not estimated. Certainly one can always use tools to rescale the raw score using score standardization (e.g., z scoring), but the person will in fact be located in relation to the sample. Thus a given person may appear to have a high ability if the rest of the sample is of low ability, and a low ability if the rest of the sample is of high ability. If, instead, we decide to keep raw scores as person estimates and decide to locate individuals based on their responses directly (for example, we decide that 50% of items succeeded is an average performance), we have a different problem: now the person's location depends on the difficulty of the items. Ideally, a person's measurement should be free from the characteristics of the instrument and from the sample collected (this relates again to the concept of measurement invariance). This is not the case in CTT.

In addition to this, a number of practical issues are difficult to solve within the CTT framework. For example, CTT assumes measurement invariance without providing (outside of factor analysis, which I previously argued is in fact an instance of IRT) a way to verify it. Further, CTT requires that a single response format is used throughout a test (i.e., we cannot mix response formats). This is also problematic if we want to use both item responses and collateral information in a psychometric model: we cannot within CTT, say, model jointly the time to respond to a remote associates test item and the time to respond to this item (or the number of times that a person changed response options). Finally, CTT does not provide a solution to account for missing item responses (again, outside of factor analysis): ideally we would be able to use the item responses of a person in scoring even when some responses are missing, while quantifying the lack of reliability resulting from such missingness.

1.5 Summary

Classical test theory is central and implicitly used in creativity research – through the use of sum/average scoring for person measurement and through the use of Cronbach's α as a measure of its reliability. However, it presents many issues in the context of measurement in general and in the context of creativity measurement in particular. Many aspects of CTT are problematic for creativity measurement, as the latter often implies multidimensional instruments (with additional factors that represent, for example, creativity domains or types of prompt, etc.), non-Gaussian item responses with nonhomogeneous errors, and item response structural relations that are by design nonlinear. Further, a number of important practical features are missing from CTT, such as person estimates that are separable from the sample and the item characteristics. These call for a more comprehensive framework, IRT, which I will now discuss.

2 Item Response Theory

2.1 Measurement through Statistical Modeling

Classical test theory provides a set of axioms that equate a score to its expectation and an error of measurement, therefore allowing us to use a set of tools (e.g., sum/average scoring). In contrast, *item response theory (IRT) – or modern test theory – is a psychological measurement framework that uses statistical modeling to explain observed item responses using unobserved characteristics of persons and items.* IRT is a framework that is useful for measurement (as we defined it earlier) because the person characteristics are estimated as part of the model and can be used to estimate the construct(s) of interest. In other words, once item responses have been collected, IRT provides a way to (attempt to) achieve person measurement. In addition, it provides methods to assess the reliability of such a measurement. If you are not familiar with IRT, you may have expected another definition. This is because IRT is often seen as primarily associated with logistic response models. Instead, IRT defines an approach that consists of using statistical modeling as a way to extract meaningful information (person measurement, test properties, etc.) from psychometric data. Where CTT directly interprets reflective measurement through the adoption and application of axioms, IRT invites us to build an appropriate statistical model – referred to as an *item response model* – that is a probabilistic explanation of the item responses. Provided that the model accurately represents the data and conceptual assumptions, it can be used for person measurement. In essence, IRT can be thought of as the statistical approach (as opposed to CTT being the axiomatic approach) to (reflective) measurement. Recognizing the distinction between CTT and IRT as a change of paradigm – from applying axioms to estimating models – is important because it allows us to understand how CTT is subsumed into IRT. Such a broad definition of IRT also allows us to better explore its scope.

2.2 Core Elements of an Item Response Model

Classical test theory (at least in its use of tau-equivalent and parallel versions) keeps person and item characteristics entangled. This means that item response models involve separate variables (or constants) that represent characteristics of items and characteristics of persons. Instead, the "ultimate defining characteristic of IRT" (van der Linden, 2016, p. 8) is that it separates person characteristics and item characteristics.

But this is only the starting point of IRT, as other variables may also be involved to represent other phenomena that affect scores (e.g., between-group factors, person covariates, item covariates, shared method factors, collateral information). In the context of this Element, however, I will primarily focus on models that involve person characteristics and item characteristics, as well as extensions that are particularly relevant in creativity research, such as extensions for rater effects and domain specificity.

In this section, after having introduced a few key elements, we will break item response models into different components. This approach will then help us build models that can adapt to the variety of situations encountered in creativity research. We will notably view models appropriate for count items (e.g., fluency scores) and response times in Section 2.2.5, models for binary responses (e.g., remote associates task item scores) in Section 2.2.6, and models for ordinal responses (e.g., self-report personality tests, consensual assessment technique creativity ratings) in Section 2.2.7.

2.2.1 Item Characteristics

Although the case for random item effects models can be made (De Boeck, 2008), in item response models, we generally think of items as having a *fixed effect* on item responses. This means that we expect a given item to always have the same effect on the responses (note that this does not imply that such an effect is estimated perfectly). For example, if we consider that item 1's only defining characteristic is its difficulty, then it has a single difficulty level to estimate. If we reuse the test or the item with any individual in the population, it is assumed to have the same level of difficulty. Although it may seem a hard sell in creativity measurement – because creativity domains can be very large and multifaceted and thus hard to sample – it is an assumption that we had already made with CTT and which IRT at least formalizes. Further, it is primarily motivated by the fact that, in general, items tend to be reused directly across studies for a given test (and not randomly resampled), while the examinees (which, as we will see, are thought of as random effects) are randomly resampled across studies.

The numbers that represent item characteristics in an item response model are generally referred to as *item parameters*. Since we consider them to be constant for a given item, for the jth item, we will note them as a_j, b_j, c_j, and so on. When estimated statistically, we generally refer to their estimates – often called *item estimates* – as $\hat{a}_j, \hat{b}_j, \hat{c}_j$, and so on.

Most of the time, the item characteristics that we want to represent as parameters are the item's difficulty (or easiness) – here noted with b_j – and discrimination (i.e., loading) – here noted with a_j (this notation is voluntarily the same as with the CTT models previously presented). In fact, most item response models will allow varying difficulty and may relax the assumption that items have equal loadings – much like the CTT models are relaxed from the essentially tau-equivalent model to the congeneric model.

The process of translation from (conceptual) item characteristics to (numeric) item parameters is often called the *parametrization* of a model. For the same characteristics, there may be equivalent parametrizations, which are, essentially, different mathematical reformulations of a model. In general, we choose parametrizations that facilitate estimation and/or interpretation. Reparametrizations are sometimes done after estimation to facilitate interpretation. To take a simple example, consider the congeneric model previously discussed (we'll only look at the structural assumption), with three alternate parametrizations:

$$\mu_{ij} = a_j\theta_i + b_j,$$
$$\mu_{ij} = a_j\theta_i - b'_j,$$
$$\mu_{ij} = a_j(\theta_i + b''_j).$$

2.2.2 Latent Variables (and Their Distributions)

We conventionally refer to person i's attribute (or *person parameter*, person characteristic) with θ_i. Because this attribute varies between persons, it is thought of as a variable, and because this variable is unobserved (but assumed to exist), it is, by definition, latent. Latent attributes may be estimated statistically: person i's estimated parameter is generally written $\hat{\theta}_i$ and often called a *person estimate*. Latent variables are conceptualized as causes of item responses. They are notably used to represent the construct(s) of interest, but they may also be used to represent other factors that have effects on the responses, such as specific/nuisance factors (rater effects, testlets, shared method variance, etc.).

In IRT, θ_i varies as a function of the person, who is randomly sampled from a population. In other words, re-collecting data will not lead to the same θ_is – because the data would not be taken from the same persons. Therefore the effect of the person on the item responses is conceptualized as a *random effect*.

Estimating an item response model requires us to formulate an assumption regarding the probability distribution of the latent variable(s) in the population – often a Gaussian distribution. To make the models identifiable (and thus estimable), we also usually fix their mean (in the population) to 0 and their variance to 1. This notably presents the convenience of making person estimates scaled like standard normal (i.e., z) scores: a score of $+1$, for example, indicates that the person is located one standard deviation above the mean. Identifying the model by fixing the latent variance (to 1) is referred to as the *variance standardization method*. An alternative is to scale the latent variable using the scale of items, by freeing the latent variance and fixing an item discrimination (to 1) – this is called the *marker method*.

By default, we typically assume that the latent variable follows a Gaussian distribution, and we will use that assumption as our starting point. To note, we separate latent variable and items here, and this normality assumption is on the attribute, not on the scores (e.g., an item response may be assumed to be Poisson distributed, while the latent variable is assumed to be Gaussian distributed). We later point to different distributional assumptions that can be made regarding latent attributes.

2.2.3 The Item Response Function

The item response function consists of the structural assumption – as opposed to the distributional assumption – of an item response model. It is the part of the model that formulates how person and item characteristics – represented respectively by person parameters $\theta_{1i}, \theta_{2i}, \theta_{3i}$, and so on, and item parameters a_j, b_j, c_j, and so on – provide an expected item response. Using our notation, we can broadly define the item response function f as:

$$E(x_{ij}) = f(\theta_{1i}, \theta_{2i}, \theta_{3i}, \ldots, a_j, b_j, c_j, \ldots).$$

For now, we will focus on unidimensional response functions (i.e., those with only one θ variable).

2.2.4 Linear Item Response Functions

If we assume that there is a linear relation between one latent variable θ_i and the expected scores, with a freely estimated slope a_j and intercept b_j, we may formulate the item response function as:

$$E(x_{ij}) = a_j\theta_i + b_j.$$

We recognize here the structural part of the congeneric model. Adding constraints to this model allows us to obtain the structural assumptions of all CTT models. Thus CTT models may be seen as unidimensional IRT models with a linear item response function and a Gaussian distributional assumption (Mellenbergh, 1994). Linear response models extend beyond CTT models, however, notably because they may be used with item distributions that are not assumed to be Gaussian. For example, we may consider a linear response model that assumes a Poisson item distribution. In addition, contrary to CTT models, the linear response model can be extended to accommodate extraneous variables (e.g., item/person covariates, additional latent variables representing nuisance factors, etc.). It is therefore important to distinguish CTT and linear response models conceptually. Nevertheless, IRT is better known for providing the possibility of using nonlinear item response functions, so let us now turn to other models that are particularly relevant in creativity research.

2.2.5 Log-Linear Item Response Functions

In creativity research, there are often situations where being more creative will provide multiplicative "returns" (i.e., the returns for being more creative are greater as creativity increases). In these situations, the rate of growth in item responses increases with the latent variable.

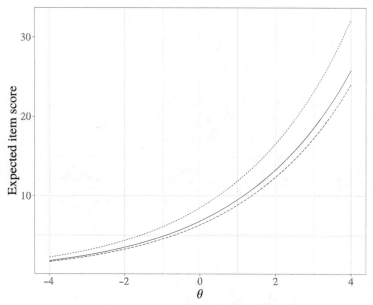

Figure 8 Expected scores of three items modeled with a 1-parameter
log-linear model

This type of construct–item response relation is multiplicative (rather than
additive, like in the linear model) and refers to the concept of *exponential
growth* (when the multiplicative factor is larger than 1). Item response models
that account for exponential growth are, for example, the Rasch Poisson count
model (RPCM), which has been used for fluency scores in divergent thinking
tasks (Baghaei & Doebler, 2019; Myszkowski & Storme, 2021). The model
may be parametrized as follows:

$$E(x_{ij}) = e^{a\theta_i + b_j}.$$

The parameter b_j represents item difficulty (or rather, easiness), and a is
a common discrimination parameter. For identification, we can either fix a
to 1 or the latent variance to 1. Using the parameters from the first items in
Myszkowski and Storme (2021), Figure 8 shows item response functions of
this model.

Two important features can be seen in this plot. First, the expected item
scores are always positive, for all items and for all ability levels. This is because
the image of the exponential function (i.e., the set of values that it can produce)
only contains positive values. Second, the item response functions never intersect. This is because the exponential function is a monotonous function and
the items only differ by their location parameter. This feature, which we have
previously mentioned, is *invariant item ordering*. It implies that the order of

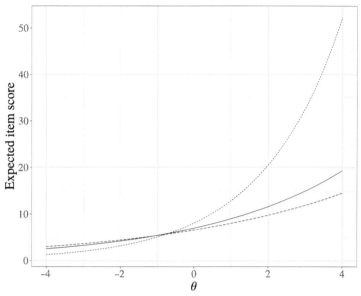

Figure 9 Expected scores of three items modeled with a 2-parameter log-linear model

item difficulties is the same for all examinees and that the order of persons with respect to their attribute θ_i is preserved in their sum/average scores for a given test (see Sijtsma & Junker, 1996; Sijtsma & van der Ark, 2017, for an introduction to the topic).

The 2-parameter Poisson counts model (Myszkowski & Storme, 2021) is a generalization of the Rasch Poisson counts model that uses an additional item parameter, a_j, to allow for items to vary in both difficulty and discrimination:

$$E(x_{ij}) = e^{a_j\theta_i + b_j}.$$

We can identify this model by freeing all a_j while fixing the latent variance to 1 (variance standardization method) or by fixing the discrimination of one item to 1 (marker method). Using the parameters from the first items in Myszkowski and Storme (2021), Figure 9 shows item response functions of this model. It can be seen that item invariant ordering is lost, as the lines now intersect.

There may be situations where we expect a more and more rapid *decrease* of expected item responses as a function of the latent trait – often referred to as *exponential decay*. This could be the case if, for example, we study the time to produce an original idea (item response) as a function of latent creativity. Figure 10 shows item response functions of such a model. These models are notably described in the literature on response time IRT (see Fox,

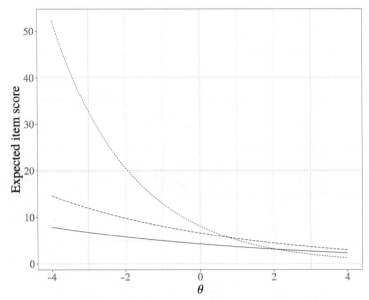

Figure 10 Expected scores of three items modeled with a 2-parameter
log-linear model (where the slopes are negative)

Klein-Entink, & van der Linden, 2007; van der Linden, 2006; van der Linden,
Klein Entink, & Fox, 2010). Whether exponential growth or decay is expected,
the same response model may be used – only the parameters will differ (more
specifically, discrimination parameters will be negative).

Employing the terminology of generalized linear models (GLMs), the exponential function, in the models discussed, may be thought of as the *inverse
link function* of the model – noted g^{-1}. The inverse link function, in a GLM
(and here as well), is the transformation applied to a linear model in order to
obtain the expectation of the outcome variable – here of an item score. Alternatively, we may formulate the same structural assumption by transforming
the other side of the equation. The function applied for such a transformation is, in the framework of GLM, called the *link function* – often noted *g*. In
log-linear response models, the link function is the natural logarithm function
$g(x) = ln(x)$.

In IRT as well as in GLM, there is no consistent convention regarding how
models are named. For example, some models are named after the item distributional assumption, after the link function, or after the inverse link function.
In the present case, it is, however, more conventional to refer to models that
use a logarithmic link function as *log-linear models* rather than as *exponential
models*.

2.2.6 Logistic Item Response Functions

As we have seen before, the exponential function is especially practical when item responses have a lower bound. We could think of the exponential function as a way to "bend" the linear model to account for such bound effects, and this analogy is particularly useful in understanding the next response model.

The practicalities of measurement often involve both an upper bound and a lower bound. Just like item scores often have a minimum, they often have a maximum as well. For example, in the case of a remote associates task or a biodata checklist coded as 0 for fail (or no) and 1 for pass (or yes), the bounds of item score distributions are 0 and 1. Similarly, if we have visual analog scales (i.e., slider scales) for creativity ratings that go from 0 to 1 (or 0% to 100%), they are also bounded. Likert scales, largely used for creativity ratings in the consensual assessment technique and for questionnaires, are also themselves limited by a lower bound and an upper bound (for them, we will, however, use a more accurate approach than the one I will discuss here).

Because of the presence of both bounds, we now need to think of "bending" the linear model twice, so that it has a lower asymptote – like the log-linear model – and an upper asymptote – unlike the log-linear model. In other words, we want an item response function that is monotonous (i.e., item responses increase or decrease as a function of the latent variable) but whose rate of increase or decrease (i.e., its slope) will tend to 0 as we approach the response bounds. What I am describing here is an S shape, often referred to as a *sigmoid*. There are several mathematical functions that can be applied to obtain a sigmoid shape. Currently, most IRT software uses the logistic function to achieve this.

Using the logistic function with a model that only allows items to vary in difficulty b_j, we obtain the 1-parameter logistic (1PL) model (often referred to as the Rasch logistic model) (Rasch, 1960), which is seen with different parametrizations and identification methods. Using a parametrization with a common a discrimination parameter, it can be expressed as:

$$E(x_{ij}) = \frac{1}{1 + e^{-(a\theta_i + b_j)}}.$$

For identification, we can again fix the latent variance and estimate a, or we can free the latent variance and fix a. Using the item parameters in Storme, Myszkowski, Baron, et al. (2019), Figure 11 shows example item response functions of this model. Using GLM terminology, the logistic function is the inverse link function, and the logit function is the link function.

Like the RPCM and the essentially tau-equivalent model (and constrained variants), the 1PL model implies invariant item ordering – which can be

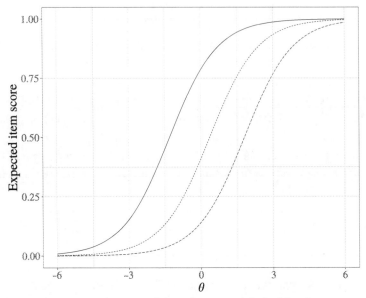

Figure 11 Expected scores of three items modeled with a 1-parameter logistic model

observed through the nonintersection of the item response functions. This implies that sum/average scores preserve the order of θ across persons, given a test. This property is lost in the next logistic models presented.

Different items frequently measure a construct with different discrimination. As argued earlier in this Element and in Myszkowski and Storme (2021), one should particularly suspect that it is the case when measuring creativity, due to (sub)domain or context specificity. The 2-parameter logistic (2PL) model (Birnbaum, Lord, & Novick, 1968) thus allows items to vary in discrimination a_j:

$$E(x_{ij}) = \frac{1}{1 + e^{-(a_j\theta_i + b_j)}}.$$

Once again, the model may be identified using the marker method or the variance standardization method. Using item parameters in Storme, Myszkowski, Baron, et al. (2019), Figure 12 shows item response functions of this model.

Since this Element is introductory, let us quickly note that the 2PL can be extended to account for guessing and slipping. The 3-parameter logistic (3PL) model adds a *pseudo-guessing parameter* g_j, which allows a varying lower asymptote. The 4-parameter logistic (4PL) model further adds a *slipping parameter* u_j, which controls the upper asymptote. The 4PL model can be written as:

$$E(x_{ij}) = g_j + \frac{u_j - g_j}{1 + e^{-(a_j\theta_i + b_j)}}.$$

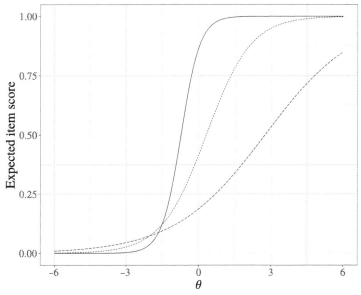

Figure 12 Expected scores of three items modeled with a 2-parameter
logistic model

The 2PL model is effectively a 4PL model with a pseudo-guessing parameter
fixed to 0 and a slipping parameter fixed to 1. Using the item parameters in
Storme, Myszkowski, Baron, et al. (2019), Figures 13 and 14 show example
item response functions of the 3PL and 4PL models, respectively.

To note, some IRT software – especially those that use Bayesian estimation
methods – also use the cumulative distribution function of the standard normal
distribution instead of the logistic function as inverse link function. In fact,
this approach was discussed for binary items prior to Rasch's seminal work on
logistic models, notably by Lord (1951). In this case, the link function is the
probit function, and the models are often referred to as *normal ogive models*.
Because of their popularity, availability, and computational efficiency, I only
discuss here approaches that use and generalize logistic models (see Albert,
2017, for a discussion on the topic).

Logistic models are widely used for binary items, but they have other uses.
For example, Doebler, Doebler, and Holling (2014) discuss how counts and
rates in many tasks have upper bounds (e.g., fluency is limited by the time taken
to write answers in divergent thinking tasks), and thus logistic models may
be used for counts and rates, notably using Poisson distributions. As another
example, Noel and Dauvier (2007) present logistic models for responses on
visual analog scales, using the beta distribution.

Creativity and Imagination

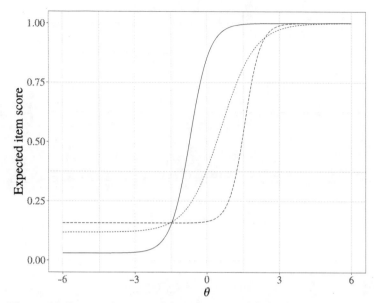

Figure 13 Expected scores of three items modeled with a 3-parameter logistic model

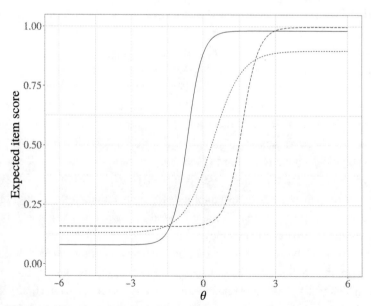

Figure 14 Expected scores of three items modeled with a 4-parameter logistic model

2.2.7 Item Response Functions for Polytomous Items

Items sometimes require persons (or raters) to select a response category from a set of more than two categories. Such items are generally referred to as *polytomous*. In some cases, the response categories are constructed and assumed to be ordered – we refer to such items as *ordinal*. We often assume an order between the categories when persons (or raters) use scales with response categories that are semantically ordered (e.g., low creativity < average creativity < high creativity).

Polytomous items require us to extend the models that we previously presented used for dichotomous items. In short, when facing polytomous items, we turn the item into a set of binary subitems (or pseudo-items), which we then model with the binary models previously discussed. More comprehensive discussions of the different models are available elsewhere (De Ayala, 2022; Ostini & Nering, 2006), and their implications for creativity research need to be further discussed, but I will summarize the main approaches.

One popular approach to polytomous data is referred to as the *divide-by-total* approach (Thissen & Steinberg, 1986). Divide-by-total models are all constrained versions of the *nominal response model* (NRM; Bock, 1972). For an item j with categories ranging from 1 to m_j, the nominal response model predicts the probability P_{ijk} that person i responds category k for item j as:

$$P_{ijk} = \frac{e^{a_{jk}\theta_i - b_{jk}}}{\sum_{h=1}^{m_j} e^{a_{jh}\theta_i - b_{jh}}}.$$

The denominator is a sum across all categories, which explains the term divide-by-total. In this model, a_{jk} represents an item-category-specific discrimination parameter for category k of item j, and b_{jk} an item-category-specific location (difficulty) parameter. Some constraints are added for identification – see Bock (1972) and Thissen and Steinberg (1986) for details. This model does not assume any order between the response categories, and it is thus suitable for nonordered polytomous items. It was originally developed for multiple choice items, as it allows information to be recovered on θ_i from distractor responses – although lesser-known alternatives, notably nested logit models (Suh & Bolt, 2010), seem to be more successful in doing so (Myszkowski & Storme, 2018; Storme, Myszkowski, Baron, et al., 2019).

The nominal response model is often thought to be too complex when we are dealing with ordinal items. Indeed, with ordinal items it is reasonable to assume that all categories equally capture the construct for a given item. The *generalized partial credit model* (Muraki, 1992) makes this additional

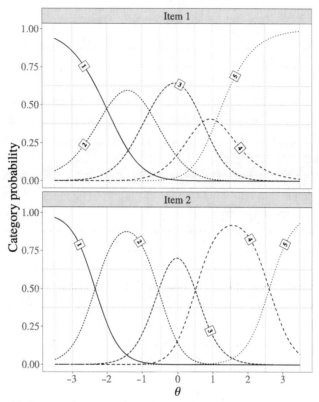

Figure 15 Expected scores of two items modeled with generalized partial credit model

assumption. Although nested within the nominal response model, it is conventionally parametrized differently: it predicts the probability that a person will respond category k over $k-1$ (e.g., choosing category 2 over 1). For categories $k = 2, 3, ..., m_j$, let us note C_{ijk} as the conditional probability of selecting k over $k - 1$ and apply the 2PL model:

$$C_{ijk} = \frac{P_{ijk}}{P_{ij,k-1} + P_{ijk}} = \frac{1}{1 + e^{-(a_j\theta_i + b_{jk})}}.$$

Conditional probabilities C_{ijk}, once modeled, are transformed to obtain probabilities for all response categories P_{ijk} (see Muraki, 1997). Item category curves represent the probability of responding a given category given θ_i. Using the example 5-point ordinal data in the package jrt, I provide example category curves in Figure 15.

The generalized partial credit model can be constrained in various ways. Notably, the *partial credit model* (Masters, 1982) constrains items to equal discrimination parameters. The (Rasch) *rating scale model* (Andrich, 1978)

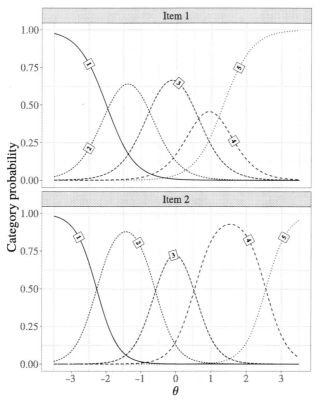

Figure 16 Expected scores of two items modeled with the graded response model

further constrains the partial credit model by fixing the category locations so that they are all spaced equally across items (i.e., items only vary by their overall location). One may also build a model that constrains category structures across items but that allows items to vary in discrimination – to the best of my knowledge, such a model is not named, but I would suggest *generalized rating scale model* (Myszkowski, 2021). Also, we may want to constrain category structures to a specific structure (for example, we may constrain them to be equally spaced between one another).

Difference models are an alternative to divide-by-total models for ordinal items (Thissen & Steinberg, 1986). They are primarily represented by the *graded response model* (Samejima, 1969), which models, using a 2PL model, the probability P^*_{ijk} that person i will respond category k or above at item j, for $k = 2, 3, \ldots, m_j$:

$$P^*_{ijk} = \frac{1}{1 + e^{-(a_j\theta_i + b_{jk})}}.$$

The probabilities P^*_{ijk} are then transformed into probabilities for each category P_{ijk}. Using the previous data, I provide example category curves for the graded response model in Figure 16. In this model, the discrimination and the thresholds between categories (i.e., the category structure) vary between items. Similarly to the generalized partial credit model, constrained versions of the graded response model can be used to constrain discrimination parameters and/or category structures so that they are equal across items. The special case of the graded response model that constrains the category structures to be the same across items (i.e., similar to the generalized rating scale model but with a different type of model) was originally discussed by Muraki (1990) and is sometimes referred to as the *graded rating scale model* (Embretson & Reise, 2000). Similarly to the generalized partial credit model, other special cases of the graded response model that constrain discriminations are also possible (Myszkowski, 2021).

Divide-by-total and difference models are not nested. This implies that we cannot employ a nested model comparison strategy (i.e., a likelihood ratio test) to compare the fit of a divide-by-total model with a difference model, but it does not mean that they are not comparable at all, as other approaches may be used (for example, the Akaike information criterion or the Bayesian information criterion).

2.2.8 Item Distributional Assumptions

Item-response theory models formulate assumptions about how the item responses – conditional upon the person attribute(s) and the item characteristic(s) (I will skip this precision throughout for brevity) – are distributed. Making an assumption about item responses is necessary in order to estimate the models, as IRT models are in general estimated using some form of maximum likelihood (ML) or Bayesian estimation procedure, which require us to formulate such an assumption.

Some models assume item responses follow a *Gaussian distribution*. This distribution is symmetric and has a continuous unbounded support. Therefore it is generally appropriate for responses that we think can be assumed to be distributed along a continuum that is unbounded. Strictly speaking, that does not happen frequently, which implies that this assumption is rarely correct. Nevertheless, it can be reasonable enough and presents advantages. For example, Likert responses are categorical, but assuming that the categories can be ordered, and with a sufficiently large number of response categories, using Gaussian linear models (i.e., traditional factor analysis) often provides reasonably good approximations for the latent attribute while also reducing the number of parameters. Simulations tend to indicate that ordinal/categorical models are most useful compared with Gaussian linear models when there are fewer categories (see Rhemtulla, Brosseau-Liard, & Savalei, 2012). Another advantage – although underused (Borsboom, 2006) – of Gaussian linear (i.e., CTT) models is that they include the models that underlie sum/average scoring (as well as Cronbach's α), as we noted. And thus by evaluating the fit of some of these models, we can – but unfortunately rarely do – provide empirical support for using CTT procedures.

Another use of the Gaussian distribution is for visual analog scales. The limit to this is that visual analog scales can be characterized by bound effects, which make distributions asymmetric and heteroscedastic (the variance shrinks as the scores approach the bounds). For this reason, distributions for continuous bounded data, like the *beta distribution*, have been presented as more appropriate with visual analog scales. Noel and Dauvier (2007) introduced, for example, 1- and 2-parameter beta response models (BRM-1 and BRM-2, respectively) that use a logistic item response function with a beta distribution.

Finally, Gaussian distributions are also used with log-linear models – this type of model, since it uses a logarithmic link function and a Gaussian distributional assumption, is often referred to as a *log-normal model*. Log-normal models are notably used in models for response times (LNIRT; Fox, Klein-Entink, & van der Linden, 2007; Fox & Marianti, 2016; van der Linden, 2006). Alternative distributions for continuous data with a lower bound have been proposed, notably including the *exponential distribution* (Mellenbergh, 1994; Rasch, 1960). Other probability distributions have been used for response times, such as the *ex-Gaussian distribution*, *ex-Wald distribution*, *gamma distribution*, and *Weibull distribution* (Hohle, 1965; Palmer, Horowitz, Torralba, et al., 2011; Schwarz, 2001), and may be alternatives to consider.

Another frequently used distributional assumption for item response models is the *Bernoulli distribution*. The Bernoulli distribution is the typical distributional assumption for binary data (e.g., remote associates task responses). Bernoulli distributional assumptions are often used with the binary logistic models presented previously. The Bernoulli distribution has one distributional parameter, the probability (often noted p or π). An interesting feature of Bernoulli distributions is that they are heteroscedastic: the variance is a function of the probability parameter ($\pi(1 - \pi)$), and more specifically, it shrinks to 0 as the probability approaches its bounds (0 and 1) and is maximized at $\pi = 0.5$. In measurement, this illustrates how a score on a binary scale is more uncertain when the probability of success approaches 0.5. To note, the Bernoulli distribution is a special case of the binomial distribution with the number of trials equal to 1, and thus the distributional assumption is sometimes referred to as

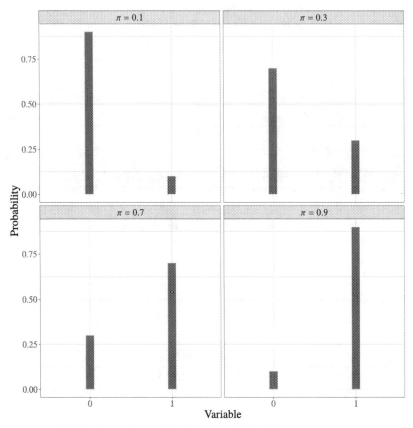

Figure 17 Bernoulli distributions for varying probability parameters

binomial when it is Bernoulli. For illustration, the probability mass function of the Bernoulli distribution with varying π is presented in Figure 17.

Categorical item response models often assume the item responses follow a *multinomial distribution*. We have, however, seen that some of these models were actually developed as adaptations of the 1PL and 2PL logistic models to dichotomized item responses. Thus such models may be thought of as models that also use the Bernoulli distribution but on subitem/pseudo-item responses. For count/rate data with no upper limit (e.g., fluency scores), models involving the *Poisson distribution* have notably been proposed (Myszkowski & Storme, 2021; Rasch, 1960; van Duijn & Jansen, 1995). The Poisson distribution is a discrete distribution that only generates positive integer values, which is appropriate for counts of events. The Poisson distribution has only one distributional parameter, the rate (noted λ), which is equal to the expectation (i.e., the mean). For illustration, the probability mass function of the Poisson distribution with varying λ is presented in Figure 18.

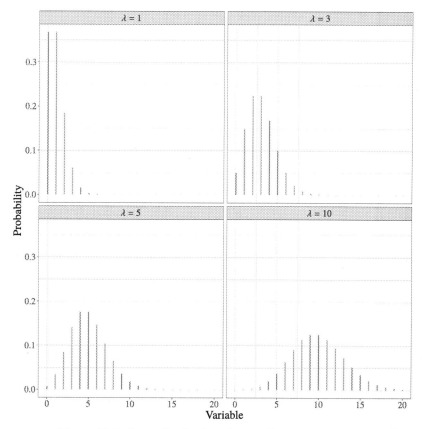

Figure 18 Poisson distributions for varying rate parameters

As can be seen in this graph, as λ increases, the distribution is not only moved to the right (i.e., larger counts are more probable), but it is also "flattened." This illustrates the fact that, in Poisson distributions, the variance is equal to (and thus increases with) the rate λ. This implies that the Poisson distribution assumes the expectation to be equal to the variance – an assumption referred to as the assumption of *equidispersion*. Violations of this assumption in item response models are frequent and have consequences – notably, reliability is overestimated in the presence of overdispersion (Baghaei & Doebler, 2019; Forthmann & Doebler, 2021). The *negative binomial distribution* has been proposed to accommodate overdispersion (the variance is larger than the expectation) (Hung, 2012), and recently the *Conwell-Maxwell-Poisson distribution* has been proposed to account for nonequidispersion in general (underdispersion and overdispersion) (Forthmann & Doebler, 2021).

Table 1 Overview of item response models available for different item types

Item type	Example distribution	Example link	Example inverse link	Example models
Continuous unbounded	Gaussian	Identity	Identity	Congeneric, parallel
Binary	Bernoulli	Logit	Logistic	1PL, 2PL, 3PL
Count (discrete with lower bound)	Poisson	Logarithm	Exponential	RPCM 2PPCM
Response time (continuous with lower bound)	Log-normal	Logarithm	Exponential	LNIRT models
Visual analog scale (continuous with lower and upper bound)	Beta	Logit	Logistic	BRM-1, BRM-2

Note: 1PL: 1-parameter logistic; 2PL: 2-parameter logistic; 3PL: 3-parameter logistic; RPCM: Rasch Poisson counts model; 2PPCM: 2-parameter Poisson counts model; LNIRT: log-normal item response theory; BRM-1: beta response model 1; BRM-2: beta response model 2.

Table 1 provides an overview of item response theory models, inspired by the table provided in Mellenbergh (1994). This overview is not exhaustive, but it demonstrates the flexibility of item response models.

2.3 Core Statistics and Diagnostics

In this section, I propose a brief overview of how models are usually estimated, how their fit is usually assessed, and how to use models to obtain person measurements.

2.3.1 Estimation

Model estimation (i.e., model fitting, model calibration) consists of using the item responses to find adequate values for the parameters of the item response model considered. In general, IRT models are estimated by finding the model parameters (i.e., the person parameters and the item parameters) so that the model is the most likely to have produced the data. This process, widely used in statistics, albeit absent from many introductory statistics classes, is known as *maximum likelihood* (ML) estimation. I will outline how ML works in general before discussing how it is implemented in IRT specifically.

First, the term *likelihood* refers to the probability of the dataset being observed, given a set of parameters. Because parameter values change the likelihood, it is discussed as a function of the parameter values and thus called the *likelihood function* – although the term *likelihood* is also used for the likelihood of the model once maximized. The objective of ML estimation is to find the set of parameter values that will maximize the likelihood function. For computational efficiency and to avoid numerical accuracy issues (a product of many probabilities is in general a very small number), we prefer to maximize the logarithm of the likelihood, or *log-likelihood*, rather than the likelihood itself.

In IRT models, ML estimation is made difficult by the need to estimate both item parameters (i.e., item difficulties, discrimination, etc.) and person parameters (i.e., a person's ability). Although this is extensively described elsewhere (e.g., De Ayala, 2022), there are two main methods to solve this problem.

Joint maximum likelihood (JML) estimation begins by using starting values for person estimates. They then are treated as known, so that we can find item parameter values that maximize the log-likelihood, given these temporary person parameter values. Once we have temporary item estimates, we in turn use them to update the person estimates by again maximizing the log-likelihood, given these temporary item estimates. We then use these new person estimates to find new item estimates and continue until the desired convergence threshold is met (i.e., when we decide that the updated parameter values do not vary too much from the previous values).

Marginal maximum likelihood (MML; Bock & Aitkin, 1982) uses a different approach. It relies on the assumption that persons are randomly sampled from a population (see the previous discussion on random and fixed effects for persons and items in Sections 2.2.1 and 2.2.2). MML estimation uses the assumed distribution of person parameters to eliminate person parameters from the estimation of item parameters. In practice, MML is an iterative process, and a popular approach for its application is the *expectation–maximization* (EM) algorithm, which is better described elsewhere (e.g., De Ayala, 2022) and which is a general approach to estimation with missing data (in this context, the person parameters are considered the missing data).

To note, a particularity of models with monotonous response functions and only one item parameter (representing difficulty), such as the 1PL and RPCM – sometimes referred to as models of the *Rasch family* (for a more thorough discussion of the term, see Rost, 2001) – is that raw (sum or average) scores are *sufficient* statistics to determine person abilities. This does not mean that knowing a person's raw score automatically tells us that person's ability level, but it means that the raw score contains all the information about it. For these models, it is possible to take advantage of this in estimation by maximizing the likelihood, conditional upon its sufficient statistics – this is referred to as *conditional maximum likelihood* (CML) estimation.

2.3.2 Person and Item Fit

Traditionally, the fit of IRT models is assessed in a piecewise manner (Maydeu-Olivares, 2013) by investigating whether the responses by a given person or to a given item are accurately predicted by the model under consideration. One approach is to examine the extent to which a person's responses are modeled accurately – that is, how close their model-implied responses and their actual observed responses are. This is known as studying *person fit*. To measure whether a person's responses are consistent with the ones predicted by the model, several indices can be used. A popular approach is to use the l_z index (Drasgow, Levine, & McLaughlin, 1987), and a corrected version of this statistic, l_z^* (Snijders, 2001), is also frequently used. I will not detail its computation here, but conceptually, this index is used to determine whether a person's set of responses is probable, given their (estimated) level. Good fit is observed when l_z is close to 0. Person fit can be used to assess the fit of the model, but it is especially relevant as a person-wise approach. This is because it allows – and is notably used for – the detection of aberrant response patterns, thus allowing the detection of a number of measurement issues (e.g., cheating, misunderstanding the items, guessing, etc.).

Alternatively, fit can be investigated item-wise. That is, we investigate the extent to which the responses predicted by the model to an item are close to the ones that were actually observed. This approach is generally referred to as *item fit* analysis. Item fit measures (and significance tests), in a nutshell, are based on the comparison between model-implied expected scores and observed scores for each item. The comparison typically results in a χ^2 statistic, which allows us to compute a p value to detect misfit. Popular methods for achieving this are the $S - X^2$ (Orlando & Thissen, 2000), the G^2 (McKinley & Mills, 1985), and the Q_1 (Yen, 1981) statistics.

2.3.3 Model Fit and Model Fit Comparisons

Some approaches have been developed to study the fit of models overall. First, models that are estimated on the same data and nested can be compared using a *likelihood ratio test* (LRT). Such a test generally takes the form of an χ^2 test, whose significance indicates that the more complex (i.e., "full" model) outperforms the least complex (i.e., "null" model).

When models are not nested but still estimated on the same dataset, it is not possible to use likelihood ratio tests, but one can still use various fit indices that penalize (log-)likelihood for model complexity. The most used are probably the *Akaike information criterion* (AIC) and *Bayesian information criterion* (BIC), along with various corrected variations on these indices. For these indices, a lower value indicates a better fit. Although these indices only indicate whether one model fits better than another accounting for its complexity, an alternate use of these indices is to transform them into *model weights* (for the AIC, they are known as *Akaike weights* and for the BIC as *Schwartz weights*). These weights, used beyond IRT (Wagenmakers & Farrell, 2004), are a way to account for the relative merits of all the tested models. In IRT, they can notably be used to decide whether, in a set of models, a subset shall be considered rather than only the best one (Myszkowski, 2021). We can also use these weights to control for Type III error (choosing the wrong model to interpret) by computing model-averaged scores or statistics where a statistic computed with various models is averaged across models, weighted using model weights (e.g., Myszkowski & Storme, 2021).

Finally, limited information goodness-of-fit measures have been developed for IRT models (Cai & Hansen, 2013; Maydeu-Olivares & Joe, 2006). They consist of computing a χ^2-distributed statistic similar to the one used to measure fit in the structural equation modeling (SEM) framework. Like in SEM, a *p* value can be used to detect a significant lack of (exact) fit. From this χ^2-distributed statistic, popular SEM fit indices, such as the Root Mean Square Error of Approximation (RMSEA), the Standardized Root Mean Square Residual (SRMR), or the Comparative Fit Index (CFI), can also be computed and used with similar decision thresholds as in SEM (e.g., Hu & Bentler, 1999).

2.3.4 Person Scoring

Joint maximum likelihood methods yield person parameter estimates directly. However, marginal maximum likelihood, the most common approach to estimating IRT models, yields only item estimates, not person estimates. To obtain them, various procedures exist. *Maximum likelihood* estimation can be performed, but it is problematic, notably because it yields infinite person estimates when the minimum or the maximum raw scores are observed. Thus we generally prefer a Bayesian strategy, which avoids such issues. This procedure combines an assumption about the person parameter distribution (e.g., that it follows a standard normal distribution) – called a prior distribution – with the information contained in a person's responses (i.e., the likelihood). This combination of the prior distribution and the data yields a distribution of a person's parameter known as the *posterior (probability) distribution* (of the person parameter estimate). To note, Bayesian IRT estimation directly yields an estimate of the posterior distribution through the parameter values of estimation chains.

Although it can be interesting to discuss a person's estimate as a probability distribution, we may instead want a point estimate. The most common approach for this step is to use the mean of the posterior distribution – doing so is referred to as computing *expected a posteriori* (EAP) estimates – or its mode – *maximum a posteriori* (MAP) estimates.

2.3.5 Information, Measurement Error, and Reliability

In psychological measurement, we want to quantify the uncertainty of the person estimates. This is captured in CTT in the concept of *reliability*, which is defined as the ratio of true score variance over the observed score variance. A common alternative – which exists similarly in CTT and IRT – consists of transforming reliability into the expected variation between measures of the same person with the test, known as the *standard error of measurement*.

In IRT, this concept is primarily defined using the concept of *information*. Fisher information – or simply information – is a way to quantify how certain we are about the value of an unknown parameter. In IRT, we study information about a person's characteristic θ_i – thus it is often written as $I(\theta_i)$. I will not detail its computation(s) here, but conceptually, information is computed based on how pointy the likelihood function (or the posterior distribution) is in the neighborhood of θ_i. If the likelihood function is very sharply peaked, then it is very sensitive to variations of θ_i, and thus we have more information on the person's location.

We can study information with various aims. *Item information* refers to the amount of information that an item provides regarding the person's attribute. *Test information* refers to the amount of information that a test provides regarding the person's attribute. A transformation can be applied to transform test information to reliability (Nicewander, 2018; Raju, Price, Oshima, et al., 2007). In essence, reliability is then thought of as a standardization of information (Raju, Price, Oshima, et al., 2007).

Apart from a different terminology, IRT brings a new, important element to the concept of reliability: conditionality. Indeed, in IRT models, information (and consequently reliability and standard error of measurement) is conditional

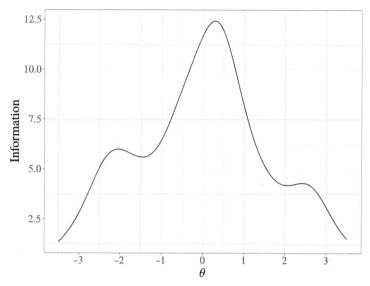

Figure 19 Test information function

upon an individual's characteristic θ. This means that individuals are measured with different degrees of precision by items (and thus by tests) depending on their attributes. This captures the intuitive notion that an item or a test that is too easy or too difficult (to succeed or agree with) will result in lower accuracy of person measurement. Because in IRT information, reliability, and standard error of measurement depend upon θ, they are studied as functions of it.

Consequently, IRT places a great emphasis on examining *item informa-tion/reliability/standard error function curves* and *test (or total) informa-tion/reliability/standard error function curves*. To illustrate this point, I show the test information and reliability functions from the generalized partial credit model earlier estimated in Figures 19 and 20, respectively.

These plots can be used to determine at which person locations an item or a test is particularly informative or lacking. However, when discussing a meas-urement instrument, it can be useful to capture reliability as a single value. Common options for this are to compute the expected reliability in the sam-ple distribution – often called *empirical reliability* – or the expected reliability in an assumed prior distribution (usually a standard normal distribution) – often referred to as *marginal reliability*. The former is more appropriate when discussing the reliability of the test in the sample, while the latter is more appropriate to infer and generalize reliability over an assumed distribution of θ. It is also possible to use bootstrapping to obtain confidence intervals (or standard errors) for reliability estimates (Myszkowski & Storme, 2018; Storme, Myszkowski, Baron, et al., 2019).

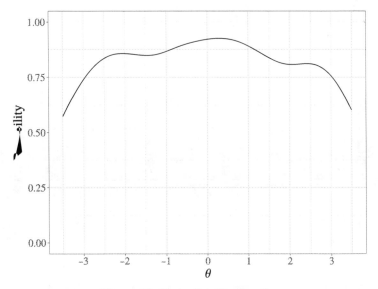

Figure 20 Test reliability function

2.3.6 Item Analysis and Selection

In IRT, each item has its own information function, which can notably be studied by looking at information function curves. Further, items are generally analyzed through plots representing expected responses as a function of the latent characteristic – these plots are generally referred to as *item (response) characteristic (function) curve* (ICC) plots. Item parameters can notably be used to make choices regarding items. Parameter estimates may also be used – we may, for example, retain items with the largest discrimination parameters. However, the complexity of many item response models generally implies that item parameters are frequently only interpretable when considering all the other parameters – and thus a graphical approach is often more useful.

Item selection procedures that do not rely on the visual inspection of ICC plots generally rely on information. Notably, *computerized adaptive testing* is a process in which the next item presented to a test taker is the optimal item to present, and such optimality is, in general, defined as the maximization of the expected information once the next item is taken. In other words, we present as the next item the item that is expected to maximize total information. Of course, other constraints may be applied, for example, to limit exposure to certain items or to create equivalent forms. Another approach that heavily relies on item information is that of *optimal test design* (see van der Linden, 2005, for a comprehensive overview). Optimal test design consists of assembling a test (or several forms of a test) in order to satisfy a number of constraints (e.g.,

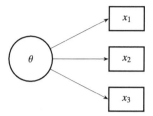

Figure 21 Conceptual representation of a unidimensional model with three items

number of items, number of items per category, etc.), while maximizing the (expected) information.

2.4 Other Assumptions and Extensions

Throughout this section, I will use as an easily generalizable example the 2-parameter Poisson counts model (2PPCM) previously introduced. We can represent conceptually the structure of this model using the path diagram in Figure 21. Responses x_{ij} for person i to item j are predicted as:

$$\lambda_{ij} = E(x_{ij}) = e^{a_j\theta_i+b_j},$$
$$x_{ij} \sim \text{Poisson}(\lambda_{ij}).$$

2.4.1 Local Independence and Unidimensionality

Like CTT models, IRT models assume that the item response is *only* caused by item characteristics and person characteristics. This means that item responses are not related to one another beyond being caused by the same person characteristic θ. This assumption is known as the assumption of *conditional independence* (or *local independence*). Further, unless otherwise specified, all item responses are assumed to be caused by a single latent trait, an assumption known as the assumption of *unidimensionality*.

There are several situations where these assumptions may be violated or questioned – it is notably the case when we have nuisance factors (i.e., shared method variance), as previously discussed. As we also discussed, in the field of creativity research we often deal with nuisance factors, which can come from rater effects or from other communalities between certain items (e.g., communalities between divergent thinking prompts).

IRT models can be extended to detect and/or account for violations of local independence and unidimensionality. For example, IRT models can allow for relations between items to exist beyond the latent attribute θ and for multiple characteristics to be measured at once (so that, for example, beyond item characteristics, both rater effects and person characteristics may be thought of as simultaneous causes of a creative product's rating).

2.4.2 Multiple Factor Models

In this section, I will discuss models where items are caused by a single latent variable but where the model includes several latent variables. In the factor analysis and structural equation modeling tradition, the multiplicity of latent variables often leads to these models being discussed as multidimensional models, but the term *multidimensional* in IRT is more traditionally used for models that also include several latent variables but where a given item can be explained by several latent variables at once (e.g., De Ayala, 2022). For clarity here, I refer to the former as *multiple factor* models and to the latter as *multidimensional* models.

Multiple factor models can be used to accommodate problems of local dependencies and/or nuisance/shared variance factors. They are essentially a combination of several unidimensional models simultaneously estimated, with various person attributes having effects on item responses. To illustrate them, imagine a situation with six divergent thinking items scored for fluency. The first three items use alternate uses prompts, while the last three are incomplete shapes with which to produce drawings. One way to account for such a situation could be to build the following multiple factor model, which uses two latent person attributes θ_{AUi} and θ_{ISi} for alternate uses and incomplete shapes, respectively. We can extend our 2PPCM structural model to a two-factor situation:

$$E(x_{1i}) = e^{a_1\theta_{AUi}+b_1},$$
$$E(x_{2i}) = e^{a_2\theta_{AUi}+b_2},$$
$$E(x_{3i}) = e^{a_3\theta_{AUi}+b_3},$$
$$E(x_{4i}) = e^{a_4\theta_{ISi}+b_4},$$
$$E(x_{5i}) = e^{a_5\theta_{ISi}+b_5},$$
$$E(x_{6i}) = e^{a_6\theta_{ISi}+b_6}.$$

In this model, we could allow the two latent variables to covary – such models are generally referred to in the psychometric literature as *correlated factors models* – although we could also constrain them to be independent – referred to as *independent* (or *orthogonal*) *factors models*. The 2-correlated-factors model for the example used is represented in Figure 22.

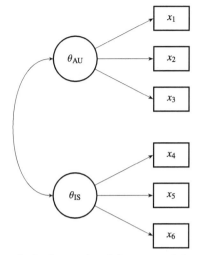

Figure 22 Conceptual of a 2-correlated-factors model model with six items

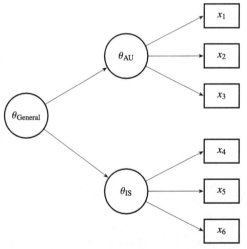

Figure 23 Conceptual representation of a hierarchical model with six items
Note: In the special case of two first-order factors (like here), this model is statistically equivalent to a 2-correlated-factors model.

It is also possible to consider the latent attributes that affect item responses as, themselves, indicators of one or several second-order factors – these models are frequently referred to as *second-order* (or hierarchical) *models*. An example second-order model is represented in Figure 23.

As we can see from the formulation of these models, they are not so different from being simultaneous IRT models estimated together. Nevertheless, they can have advantages in certain situations. For one, the relations between

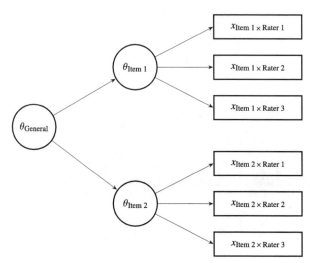

Figure 24 Conceptual representation of a hierarchical rater model for two items and three raters

the latent attributes may facilitate/stabilize the estimation of parameters, compared with estimating models separately. This is because if the two abilities are correlated, the information obtained for one helps us gain information on the other (and vice versa). Second, estimating such models allows us to estimate (and thus discuss) the correlations between the attributes at the latent level – in this example, such a model could be used to study the relation between alternate uses fluency and incomplete shapes fluency.

In the example of designs involving multiple raters and multiple items (i.e., persons respond to multiple items, which are rated by multiple raters) – common in designs involving the consensual assessment technique – it is possible to use a hierarchical model, where an item-by-rater response for an examinee is predicted by a latent variable representing an examinee's latent attribute for the item – often referred to as a true rating factor – and where true rating factors are all caused by a second-order factor, representing the examinee's attribute (generalized across all items). Such models are generally referred to as *hierarchical rater models* (Patz, Junker, Johnson, et al., 2002).

To note, it is often the case that the same raters are involved in rating all items (i.e., in this example, raters 1, 2, and 3 are the same for both items). The hierarchical rater model unfortunately does not account for dependencies between responses observed from the same rater (e.g., dependency between $x_{\text{Item 1} \times \text{Rater 1}}$ and $x_{\text{Item 2} \times \text{Rater 1}}$) (Robitzsch & Steinfeld, 2018). Fortunately, this is possible with compensatory models, which are discussed next.

Overall, multiple factor models can be used to accommodate several situations relevant in creativity research, and they have the advantage of being composed of multiple unidimensional models at the item (or item-by-rater) response level. Thus even if a piece of software is not capable of estimating models with complex factor structures, the model can be broken into pieces. For example, in the hierarchical rater model presented in Figure 24, it is possible to first estimate a model with item 1 responses, which will yield estimates for $\theta_{\text{Item }1i}$, then estimate a model with item 2 responses, which will yield estimates for $\theta_{\text{Item }2i}$. Finally, one can obtain estimates of the general $\theta_{\text{General}i}$, by using a congeneric model with $\theta_{\text{Item }1i}$ and $\theta_{\text{Item }2i}$ treated as indicators. Although a piecemeal approach to estimating a model appears suboptimal, it presents the advantage of facilitating the detection of partial (mis)fit in certain parts of the model. For example, in a hierarchical rater model, it can allow the detection of items that present strong discrepancies between raters (which can be detected though item fit, applied at the item-by-rater level). In addition, a piecemeal approach may be used to obtain good starting values that will facilitate the estimation of a larger model.

2.4.3 Multidimensional Compensatory Models

In some cases, a response can be explained by several latent person attributes at once. Let us keep our previous divergent thinking example (with alternate uses and incomplete shapes): we could think of the response as a reconciliation of multiple latent factors that may compensate one another. This is formulated through *multidimensional compensatory models*.

If we are interested in a general factor of fluency across domains, we could estimate a model where responses are simultaneously caused by a person's general fluency and by their domain- (or prompt-) specific fluency. Using our previous terminology, we could write such a model as:

$$E(x_{1i}) = e^{a_1\theta_{\text{General}i}+a_1'\theta_{\text{AU}i}+b_1},$$

$$E(x_{2i}) = e^{a_2\theta_{\text{General}i}+a_2'\theta_{\text{AU}i}+b_2},$$

$$E(x_{3i}) = e^{a_3\theta_{\text{General}i}+a_3'\theta_{\text{AU}i}+b_3},$$

$$E(x_{4i}) = e^{a_4\theta_{\text{General}i}+a_4'\theta_{\text{IS}i}+b_4},$$

$$E(x_{5i}) = e^{a_5\theta_{\text{General}i}+a_5'\theta_{\text{IS}i}+b_5},$$

$$E(x_{6i}) = e^{a_6\theta_{\text{General}i}+a_6'\theta_{\text{IS}i}+b_6}.$$

This type of compensatory model is often referred to as a *bifactor* or *testlet model* – where each response is predicted by a general and a specific factor. We can represent it conceptually in Figure 25.

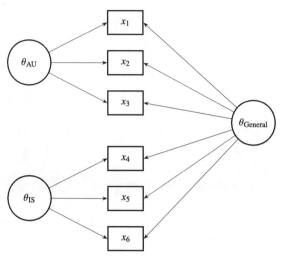

Figure 25 Conceptual representation of a bifactor (compensatory) model
with six items

As we saw previously, the hierarchical rater model did not allow the modeling of dependencies within raters and items at the same time, and in general in this model dependencies are modeled within items only (Robitzsch & Steinfeld, 2018). With compensatory models, we can now simultaneously model rater and item effects while estimating a general person attribute. In this context, items and raters may be seen as having specific effects to control for, as in Figure 26.

This type of model is referred to as a generalized many-facets model (GMFM) – see Barbot, Kaufman, and Myszkowski (2023) for an example application on creativity ratings. In this model, item category response probabilities are simultaneously predicted by item difficulty, rater severity, and person ability. This model should not be confused with the many-faceted Rasch model (MFRM), which is essentially a Rasch unidimensional model applied on the combinations rater by item (Robitzsch & Steinfeld, 2018). While the MFRM allows item difficulties to vary by rater, it does not model local dependencies within rater or item.

Another application of compensatory models is *exploratory models*, where we generally use a number of latent variables (between one and the total number of items) to simultaneously explain all item responses. This type of model is typically used to decide on the factor structure of instruments. For illustration, I represent an exploratory model with four items and four latent factors extracted in Figure 27. Strategies for exploring factor structures in the IRT tradition are discussed in Section 3.3.

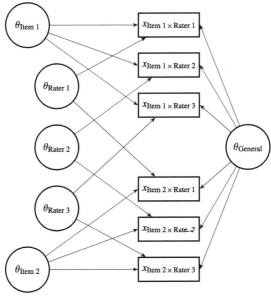

Figure 26 Conceptual representation of a testlet (i.e., generalized many-facets) rater model with three raters and two items

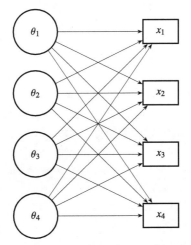

Figure 27 Conceptual representation of an exploratory model with four items

In sum, we could think of compensatory models as a generalization of unidimensional models. While unidimensional response models are expressed with a single latent attribute θ_i and a single discrimination parameter a_j by item, multidimensional response models are written with several latent variables θ_{1i}, θ_{2i}, and so on and several slope parameters a_1, a_2, and so on. Considering

2-parameter models, we have, for an item j, case i, and inverse link function g^{-1}, the following general formula for a multidimensional compensatory model with l latent factors:

$$E(x_{ij}) = g^{-1}(a_{1j}\theta_{1i} + a_{2j}\theta_{2i} + \ldots + a_{lj}\theta_{li} + b_j).$$

This type of generalization is very similar to the generalization of simple regression models to multiple regression models, in that we replace a product slope × predictor by a linear combination of l slopes and l predictors (but of course, here, the major difference is that the predictors are latent). Let us add that multiple factor models, described earlier, can be seen as particular cases of multidimensional compensatory models, where, for a given item, only one of the slope parameters is nonnull.

As a side note, other approaches have been developed for situations where several latent variables cause a single item, which are referred to as *noncompensatory models* and not discussed here because they are quite rarely seen and generally harder to estimate (De Ayala, 2022).

2.4.4 Measurement Invariance and Differential Item Functioning

Although we commonly assume Gaussian distributions for latent variables, we sometimes suspect that the population being studied is heterogeneous. Furthermore, we may suspect that the items function differently (e.g., with different difficulties) per subpopulation. For example, say we measured the musical creativity of $1,000$ individuals and we recorded whether they play a musical instrument or not. We could presume that the population is heterogeneous, and we may want to ensure that the instrument functions in similar ways for the two groups. The assumption that an instrument functions in the same way for all is referred to as the assumption of *measurement invariance* and is a key assumption in psychometrics.

In the framework of IRT, to study measurement invariance we would resort to a set of procedures referred to as *differential item functioning* (DIF) analysis. DIF analysis essentially consists of a series of model comparisons involving multigroup IRT models. For these comparisons, common practice is to first estimate with a model where the groups differ in item parameters. This is often referred to as the *configural invariance model*. If this model provides a sufficient fit (and/or sufficient fit in the groups separately), we would assume configural invariance and would then proceed to add equality constraints between models. We generally first add a constraint that equates item discrimination parameters across groups. This is referred to as the *metric* (i.e., *weak*) *invariance model*. If this model does not hold, we refer to the items as

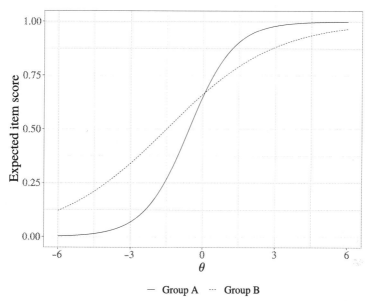

Figure 28 An item exhibiting nonuniform DIF in a logistic response model

presenting *nonuniform DIF* (see Figure 28 for an illustration). If it holds, we usually further constrain the difficulty parameters to be equal across groups: this is referred to as the *scalar* (i.e., *strong*) *invariance model*. If this model does not hold, while the weak invariance model does (i.e., the items only differ in difficulty), we say that the items present *uniform DIF* (see Figure 29 for an illustration). Once item parameters have been constrained, we might then study various constraints on the latent means and variances, allowing us to study group mean (and variance) differences. If a model with equal means further improves model fit, we conclude there are no mean differences between groups. In general, the latent mean comparison is thought to be only meaningful when strong invariance is achieved.

A common issue with the strategy above is that the least constrained models might not be easy to calibrate (or might be nonidentified) due to the number of parameters to estimate on group sizes that may not (all) be large enough. An alternative strategy consists of first fitting a model that assumes strong invariance (i.e., equal item parameters but free latent mean and variances). From there, equality constraints can be released and tested (e.g., with a likelihood ratio test or using criteria like the AIC) for each item (or in blocks) separately (see Thissen, Steinberg, & Gerrard, 1986) or in sequence (i.e., in a stepwise manner).

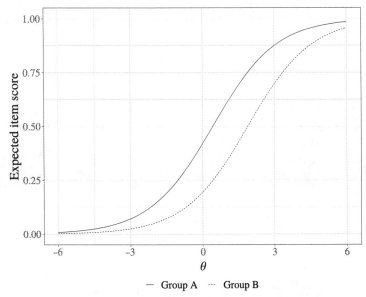

Figure 29 An item exhibiting uniform DIF in a logistic response model

The model comparison approach is very flexible, as it is applicable to virtually all measurement models. Nevertheless, we should also note that approaches that are not based on IRT model fit comparisons have been developed (especially for binary items), such as the Mantel–Haenszel χ^2 test and the logistic regression approach (see De Ayala, 2022, for an overview).

In the same way that the congeneric (i.e., traditional CFA) model can be thought of as a particular case of IRT, multigroup CFA, which is used for the study of measurement invariance in the structural equation modeling framework, can be thought of as a particular case of DIF analysis. However, in contrast with how measurement invariance is usually investigated in the CFA tradition, it is conventional to study DIF in IRT at the item level rather than on the level of the instrument as a whole.

2.4.5 Explanatory Models

Beyond being interested in how an item may function differently across populations of persons, one may, more generally, be interested in how item parameters (especially item difficulties) and/or person parameters (a person's level) may be influenced by different variables. Let us use the example of a set of ratings of the creativity of stories produced by a set of participants. On the examinee side, we could speculate that verbal ability, which perhaps has been measured, influences an examinee's latent level. We would describe verbal ability as a *person covariate*.

Further, imagine that the raters either have a degree in creative writing or are novice raters. We could speculate that, for any given product, novice raters would be more "easily impressed," and thus we would expect them to be less severe. In other words, if we consider judges as items (Myszkowski & Storme, 2019), we could build a model that studies the effect of *item (or judge) covariates*.

The study of person and item covariates in IRT models is generally referred to as *explanatory IRT*. The most common models discussed for studying item covariates are certainly the *linear logistic test model* (LLTM; Fischer, 1973) and its random item extension (LLTM+e; De Boeck, 2008). To study person covariates, the most common approach is generally referred to as a *latent regression*. Models and procedures for such investigations are notably presented in De Boeck (2011).

2.4.6 Latent Class and Mixture Models

Differential item functioning analysis is useful when it is suspected that a test functions differently by group. But what if a group effect is suspected but the variable has not been measured? For example, what if the individuals responding to our musical creativity instrument are using different generating strategies (probably with different efficiency), unbeknownst to us? This would create a heterogeneous population of persons, which we would need to disentangle.

In such cases, we may not want to assume that the overall pooled distribution of the latent variable forms a Gaussian distribution in the population but that it is instead a combination of a number of several distributions. These distributions are usually assumed to be Gaussian themselves but may vary in mean, variance, and weight in the overall population (in our example, one generation strategy may be used by more persons than another). These are referred to as (finite) *mixture distributions*, and the associated models are referred to as *mixture models*. Mixture models with continuous (normal) observed variables (i.e., item responses) are frequently referred to as *latent profile analysis* models, while mixture models with categorical observed variables are frequently referred to as *latent class analysis* models. Technically, however, both assume persons belong to unobserved (latent) classes.

To note, it is also possible to assume that the latent variable is not a mixture of Gaussian distributions but a categorical variable. This is generally referred to as a *discrete latent class model*. In these models, in contrast with mixture

Table 2 Summary of the main different assumptions of an IRT model

IRT model component	Example assumption (2PL model)
Item response distribution	Bernoulli
Latent attribute distribution	Gaussian
Response functional form	Logistic
Item parameters	Difficulty (intercept) and discrimination (slope)
Structural model	One latent trait (unidimensional structure)
Local dependencies	None
Population composition	Homogeneous
Item covariates	None

models, persons within a class are assumed not to vary in the psychological attribute measured (i.e., each class is completely homogeneous).

For discrete latent class and mixture models, it is common to estimate a series of models with varying numbers of classes. Models can be compared in fit to decide on the number of classes. Then, because the classes are unobserved, we generally want to interpret the classes, using, for example, their parameters (e.g., latent means) or their relations with other variables.

In sum, like any model, an IRT model is made of a set of assumptions about how item responses have occurred. In Table 2, I summarize the different assumptions discussed in this section.

3 Building a Modeling Strategy

In this section, I aim to provide researchers and test developers with a strategic approach to modeling test data. The stages introduced here, and summarized in Figure 30, represent a suggested – but not necessarily prescribed – course of action when planning the IRT analysis of measurement data.

3.1 Identifying Item Score Distributions

As a first step, I suggest that researchers consider the type of item response they are faced with in order to select a distributional assumption. I previously discussed the main different item distributions, but how to choose between them?

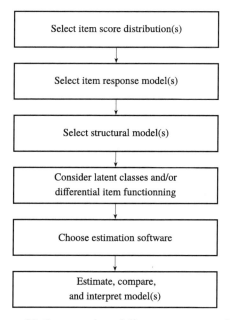

Figure 30 Suggested modeling strategy overview

Perhaps the most important aspect here is to review possible observations for an item. Are there two possibilities (e.g., pass–fail test, yes/no answers)? If so, I would suggest going for Bernoulli models. Are the responses ordinal (e.g., Likert scales, ordinal rating scales)? If so, choose adaptations of Bernoulli models for ordinal data. Are responses located in an unbounded (or at least an without severe bound effects) continuum (or at least an interval with many response categories)? If so, I would suggest Gaussian models. Are the responses discrete counts that have no known upper bound (e.g., fluency scores)? If so, choose distributions of the Poisson family (or variations). If they have a known bound (e.g., count of occurrences in a given number of trials), then use a binomial distribution. Are responses continuous but with a lower bound (e.g., response times)? If so, a log-normal or a gamma distribution would be appropriate.

Choosing a distribution first is not always easy, but the idea is to first be guided by what the scores will or do "look like." Sometimes several distributions may be considered as plausible assumptions for the same dataset. Choosing one should be substantiated conceptually and/or empirically (for example, by investigating model residuals) whenever possible. From there, the candidate set of models should be narrowed down substantially.

To note, although it is common for a test to consist of items that all have the same response format – and thus for which the same score distribution can be assumed – it is also possible to build instruments that have items with different response formats.

3.2 Identifying Item Response Functions

Once an item score distribution has been identified for an item, a set of items, or an entire test, I recommend choosing a response model. Assuming a distribution, the choice of a response model is usually already restricted, but it can still be quite broad.

I would suggest at this point first looking for typical models used for the response distribution – for example, the ones presented in this Element, or in other IRT textbooks. As I noted earlier, common item response functions typically represent the constraints in the range of item scores. For example, since binary (or visual analog scale) items have expected responses with a lower and an upper bound, a logistic function is used to constrain expected scores within these bounds.

Items are generally thought to primarily differ in difficulty (their typical location) and discrimination (the strength and direction of their relation to the construct). As a result, these item characteristics are the ones conventionally considered (e.g., the congeneric linear model, the 2-parameter logistic model), regardless of the form of the response function. Usually, simpler 1-parameter versions are considered (typically by assuming equal discrimination). Beyond this, different parameters may be introduced to represent various ways in which items can differ (e.g., guessing, category structures, etc.).

Note that once a distribution is assumed for the item scores, it is relatively easy to compare response models using various strategies, such as likelihood ratio tests (if the models are nested) or deviance information criteria (AIC, BIC, etc.). Consequently, it is advisable to retain a set of candidate response models, rather than one model, and to compare them empirically.

3.3 Identifying Structural Models

As noted, there are many situations that call for multidimensional models or for suspecting that the assumption of local independence may be violated. Different strategies may be adopted here.

First, a set of candidate structures may be narrowed down from the anticipated test structure. For example, say we are dealing with a measurement that attempts to measure creativity using three subtests, we may envision a unidimensional model (local dependencies within subtests are ignored), a 3-correlated-factors model (i.e., multiple factor model), a hierarchical (i.e., second-order) model, and a bifactor (i.e., compensatory) model. In such cases, it is common to estimate this set of models and to compare them empirically and select the best-fitting model.

If the structure of the instrument is unknown (or if it is suspected that the candidate models identified could insufficiently represent the structure of the item responses), one may turn to exploratory models in order to identify a suitable structure. Although the typical tools of exploratory factor analysis (e.g., parallel analysis, scree plots) are not usually implemented in IRT packages, one can in general easily (provided that compensatory models can be estimated) use a strategy that consists of first estimating a unidimensional model and then adding latent factors stepwise (comparing models with likelihood ratio tests or information criteria like the AIC or BIC). This approach to dimensionality assessment has been referred to as *full-information item factor analysis* (Bock, Gibbons, & Muraki, 1988).

Considering that eigenvalues – which are the main indices analyzed in traditional factor analysis to decide on the number of factors to retain – represent conceptually the explanatory power of the extracted factors, an alternative procedure for dimensionality investigation in IRT is to replace them in analysis (e.g., scree test, parallel analysis) by some other measure of explanatory power available in IRT (e.g., the sum of squared loadings or the proportion of variance explained). Spurious factors would be expected to yield values for these metrics that are substantially different (e.g., a lower sum of squared loadings and lower proportion of variance explained) from nonspurious factors, hopefully allowing for informed decision-making regarding dimensionality. Additionally, let us note that traditional factor analysis methods can be used on other measures of item association than correlations, such as polychoric correlations.

Another possibility to further one's understanding of the structure of an instrument, and to potentially uncover a different structure than initially thought, is to look for local dependencies. This essentially consists of investigating (and possibly significance testing) the relations between the residuals of item response models (Chen & Thissen, 1997). From the relations between the residuals, it is sometimes possible to refine a measurement model to better account for specific factors.

Finally, if the purpose of dimensionality assessment is to verify that the structure of an instrument is sufficiently unidimensional, the DETECT procedure (Stout, Habing, Douglas, et al., 1996) can be used. This procedure, more extensivly discussed elsewhere (Bonifay, Reise, Scheines, et al., 2015), results in an index that indicates the extent to which an item departs from essential unidimensionality. DETECT indices for each item can be compared with reference values for weak, moderate, and strong multidimensionality (Roussos & Ozbek, 2006).

3.4 Considering Latent Classes and Differential Item Functioning

Most person attributes studied in creativity research are routinely assumed to follow a normal distribution in a homogeneous population. Thus, like in most

IRT introductions, I chose not to discuss this aspect extensively. Nevertheless, I consider that this is an appropriate stage at which to consider whether the latent variable(s) identified in the previous step can be assumed to be continuous, to be comprised of a set of discrete classes (ordered or not), or to be a mixture of distributions, within which the variable follows a random (usually Gaussian) distribution.

Further, if it is suspected that an observed group variable may play an important role in how the test functions, or if it is of substantive interest to compare groups, it is appropriate to consider studying DIF or explanatory IRT models at this stage.

3.5 Fitting and Comparing Models

The next stage consists of identifying how to estimate models, as well as how to extract information about them (e.g., parameters, reliability, model diagnostics, model fit indices, model comparisons, plots). In general, this is done using the same package, but not necessarily. Notably, it is common to use a package for estimation and a different package for plotting IRFs and ICCs (see for example Myszkowski & Storme, 2021, where Mplus is used for estimation and ggplot2 is for plotting).

This Element does not intend to present an exhaustive list of packages and methods, but there are now many packages capable of estimating IRT models. First, a number of general-purpose statistical analysis software packages include IRT procedures. For example, Stata currently supports popular models for binary, ordinal, and categorical items and provides several tools for plotting. Through generalized structural equation modeling, it can also fit other models, such as linear and log-linear models. Mplus is more oriented towards structural equation modeling, but it can fit models for binary, ordinal, and categorical outcomes, as well as models for response times and count outcomes. Some commercial software packages are also dedicated to IRT analysis and present dedicated features, like XCalibre, flexMIRT, or IRTPRO, which fit the most popular models for binary and ordinal data. There are also many packages available for open-source statistical programming languages – especially R. The most popular R packages for IRT are probably mirt (Chalmers, 2012) and ltm (Rizopoulos, 2006). Although it is a structural equation modeling package, lavaan (Rosseel, 2012) can fit linear response models as well as models for binary and categorical data. For 1-parameter (Rasch) models specifically, the package eRm (Mair & Hatzinger, 2007) is also popular, as well as packages used for multilevel modeling, such as lme4 (Bates, Mächler, Bolker, et al., 2015) (see Boeck, Bakker, Zwitser, et al., 2011, for a tutorial). To conclude this nonexhaustive list, the package brms (Bürkner, 2017) provides an interface for general Bayesian modeling in Stan that accommodates IRT models (see Bürkner, 2020, for a tutorial).

4 Example Applications

In this section, I propose example applications of IRT models in the field of creativity research. The goal is to illustrate the feasibility and benefits of IRT modeling in this field.

4.1 Modeling Divergent Thinking Fluency Scores

This first example is a tutorial adaptation of a paper discussing the 2-parameter Poisson counts model (Myszkowski & Storme, 2021). It reuses an open dataset previously published (Silvia, Winterstein, Willse, et al., 2008) and proposes different analyses of the fluency scores of different items. The part of the test that we are concerned with (which I will simply refer to as "the test") consists of six items. The items prompt for alternate uses of a brick and of a knife, for consequences of people no longer having to sleep and of everyone shrinking to be 12 inches tall, and for instances of round objects and of things that make a noise. We are using as item scores the count of ideas generated for each task. The goal of this measurement is to measure divergent thinking fluency.

4.1.1 Identifying a Candidate Item Distribution

Since item scores here are counts of ideas, the responses are integer and have a lower bound of 0 and no upper bound (this is not strictly true, since even with a very high creativity, the item response is in fact limited by the number of ideas that one can write, say, or type). Although other distributions may be considered (e.g., the negative binomial distribution), the Poisson distribution seems appropriate, as it presents similar features to the item response. We will choose it here:

$$x_{ij} \sim \text{Poisson}(\lambda_{ij}).$$

Now that we have a distributional assumption for our response model, we will turn to the structural assumption, starting with the response function and then discussing the structure.

4.1.2 Identifying a Candidate Response Function

For now, let us temporarily assume that the test is unidimensional, meaning that all item scores are caused by a single latent attribute, which we will refer to as θ_i. We will also assume that the shape of the relation between θ_i and the rate of ideas produced is of exponential shape (that is, the rate of ideas is multiplied as fluency increases). Regarding item parameters, we will consider successively a model where items are perfectly interchangeable (log-linear parallel model), a model where items differ in difficulty (log-linear Rasch model), and a model where items differ in difficulty and discrimination (log-linear 2-parameter model) – the latter two models are the Rasch Poisson counts model (RPCM) and the 2-parameter Poisson counts model (2PPCM), respectively.

The three models are nested. To facilitate interpretation, we will express them as variants of the 2PPCM. The models are all identified by the variance standardization method (the latent variance is fixed to 1). In the 2PPCM model, for an item j and person i:

$$E(x_{ij}) = \lambda_{ij} = e^{a_j \theta_i + b_j}.$$

a_j corresponds to the discrimination parameter, while b_j corresponds to the difficulty parameter. In the RPCM, we constrain all discriminations to be equal to a unique discrimination a:

$$E(x_{ij}) = \lambda_{ij} = e^{a \theta_i + b_j}.$$

The log-linear parallel model further constrains all difficulty parameters to be equal to a unique difficulty parameter b:

$$E(x_{ij}) = \lambda_{ij} = e^{a \theta_i + b}.$$

We will assume that this set of candidate response models contains an accurate representation of the data. Let us now turn to dimensionality.

4.1.3 Identifying Candidate Structures

Regarding dimensionality, the measurement situation seems to call for various alternate structures. First, we may suspect that items are caused by a single latent trait (representing fluency). Based on the 2PPCM, we have:

$$E(x_{ij}) = \lambda_{ij} = e^{a_j \theta_i + b_j}.$$

As we have seen, however, different types of prompts are used in the measure – alternate uses, consequences, and instances. Thus we may suspect the presence of local dependencies (i.e., violations of local independence). In the original paper (Myszkowski & Storme, 2021), we propose to account for these nuisance factors by using a bifactor model – referred to as the bifactor 2-parameter Poisson counts model (B2PPCM). This model is a compensatory multidimensional model, which extends the 2PPCM by adding a specific/nuisance factor for each item. For an item of a given specific category, we can write the B2PPCM as a function of the general factor θ_i, specific factor θ_i', item difficulty b_j, general item discrimination a_j, and specific item discrimination a_j':

$$E(x_{ij}) = \lambda_{ij} = e^{a_j\theta_i + a_j'\theta_i' + b_j}.$$

The specific factor θ_i' depends on the type of prompt. For identification, the variance of all latent traits is fixed to 1.

To note, it would also be possible to create constrained versions of the B2PPCM with a constraint of equality on all general a_j discrimination parameters (we could perhaps refer to it as a Rasch-general B2PPCM, or RG-B2PPCM), constraints of equality across specific parameters a_j' for each item cluster (Rasch-specific B2PPCM, or RS-B2PPCM), or both (Rasch-general-specific B2PPCM, or RGS-B2PPCM). These were not originally investigated – and rarely are – and for the sake of brevity we will not discuss them here.

4.1.4 Identifying Software

Based on our current set of models, we need to use software that can fit log-linear Poisson response models, which typical IRT-dedicated software rarely does (most are focused on binary and polytomous item responses). We also need to fit a model with variable discrimination parameters, which excludes some generalized multilevel modeling software that can only fit Rasch models, such as lme4. Generalized SEM packages, such as Stata or Mplus, appear ideal in this situation. In the original paper (Myszkowski & Storme, 2021) we used Mplus – the syntax for running the models is provided as supplemental material of the paper.

4.1.5 Application

The comparison of models is further detailed in Myszkowski and Storme (2021), but I will briefly summarize it here. We compared the different models using likelihood ratio tests and information criteria and found that the log-linear parallel model was outperformed by the RPCM, which was outperformed by the 2PPCM, which was outperformed by the B2PPCM.

4.1.6 Benefits of IRT

Using these models allows us to account for multiple characteristics of the measurement situation – the distribution of the outcome, the exponential shape of the trait–item relation, and the item specificities – their difficulty, their relation to the trait, and their relation to the specific factors. Being able to control for all of these simultaneous effects leads to a measurement model that is more accurate – as evidenced by the increase in fit. Had we used an

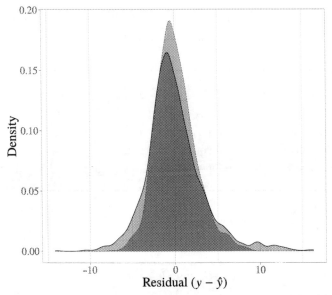

Figure 31 Distribution of residuals for an average score model (plain line) vs. the best-fitting IRT model (dashed line)

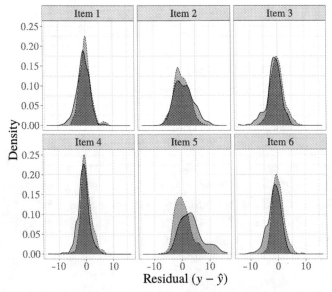

Figure 32 Distribution of residuals for an average score model (plain line) vs. the best-fitting IRT model (dashed line)

average or a sum score instead, we would have (implicitly) assumed, instead, the tau-equivalent linear model, which we know to be incorrect (be it only for predicting noninteger and negative scores, which we know to be impossible).

Although not presented in the article (Myszkowski & Storme, 2021), we can be more confident of the accuracy by looking at the distribution of the residuals of our best-fitting IRT model here (the B2PPCM) and comparing it with the distribution of residuals for average scoring. In Figures 31 and 32, we can see that the IRT model produces residuals closer to 0, overall in the test and for each item specifically, thus demonstrating a gain in accuracy. To assess the typical distance between observed and predicted scores, we may use the root mean squared error (RMSE), which is the square root of the mean squared error between predictions and observations, and the mean absolute error (MAE) – lower values indicate smaller errors and thus improved predictions. The RMSE was 3.35 when using average scores and 2.33 when using IRT (with the B2PPCM) – over 30% (or 1.02 ideas) in error reduction. A similar pattern was found for the MAE, which dropped from 2.43 to 1.80.

On a practical level, after fitting these models, it is possible to extract person estimates. This gives us a measure of fluency that, ultimately, accounts for all the previously discussed characteristics. In addition, it is notably possible to extract standard errors of measurement for each person estimate differentially – which is also an important gain from using IRT – while also obtaining a group-level reliability estimate (reliability for the entire sample), which can then be used to judge of the reliability of the measurement device.

4.2 Modeling Ordinal Ratings from the Consensual Assessment Technique

In this second example, we will focus on a central paradigm in creativity: the consensual assessment technique (CAT; Amabile, 1982). As previously discussed, it consists of asking different examinees to produce ideas (in some cases multiple prompts may be used). Afterwards, judges rate them on a set of criteria – such as creativity, originality, elaboration, or aesthetic quality.

Typically, ratings are collected on ordinal Likert scales. For the sake of simplicity here, we are going to assume a situation with multiple judges but only one prompt. Models, however, exist to accommodate situations with multiple judges and multiple items that are based on the IRT tradition (Barbot, Kaufman, & Myszkowski, 2023; Primi, Silvia, Jauk, et al., 2019; Robitzsch & Steinfeld, 2018). Moreover, as previously discussed, approaches more rooted in (generalized) structural equation modeling, such as the bifactor model, can be used as well – they essentially consist of using different latent variables representing items and judges to account for local dependencies induced by items and raters simultaneously.

Table 3 Planned missingness design ("x" indicates that the judge has judged the case's production)

Case	Judge 1	Judge 2	Judge 3	Judge 4	Judge 5
1 through 50	x	x			x
51 through 100			x	x	x
151 through 200		x		x	x
201 through 250	x			x	x
251 through 300		x	x		x
300 through 350	x	x	x	x	x

I will use for this example a simulated dataset from the package jrt (Myszkowski, 2021). The data consists of 350 products (each from a different person) rated by 5 judges. A planned missingness design is used, where all possible pairs of judges among judges 1 through 4 each judge 50 products, while all products are rated by judge 5 – the *anchor judge* – and the products of the 50 persons – *anchor persons* – are judged by all judges. The judge/case coverage is presented in Table 3.

4.2.1 Identifying a Candidate Item Distribution

Since the scales are ordinal in this example, we break down the ordinal response into binary responses. As discussed previously, there are two approaches to this: the divide-by-total approach (for ordinal models, the models that use this approach are the generalized partial credit model and its constrained versions) and the difference approach (for ordinal models, the models that use this approach are the graded response model and its constrained versions). Both break down items into sets of binary pseudo-items, which are assumed to follow Bernoulli distributions.

4.2.2 Identifying a Candidate Response Function

For binary (pseudo-)items, it is typical to use logistic models, which we will use here. Both families of models allow various features to vary by item. They can allow items to vary in overall item difficulty – here this translates into judge severity – item discrimination – or here judge discrimination – and response category structures (i.e., distances between response category thresholds).

For the sake of brevity, we are going to narrow down our response model search to the divide-by-total category of models, and we will consider models with judges that vary only in difficulty (Rasch rating scale model), in difficulty and category structure (partial credit model), and finally in difficulty, category structure, and discrimination (generalized partial credit model, our generating model here).

4.2.3 Identifying Candidate Structures

For this example, we assume that there are no local dependencies between ratings apart from the dependencies induced by different raters and different examinees. Thus we assume a unidimensional structure.

Again, typical explorations in structure here would be recommended if it were suspected that there could be local dependencies induced by having several items and/or several rubrics/judging criteria (see previous discussions on accommodating for these situations).

4.2.4 Identifying Software

Here we are using a unidimensional model but considering several response models. Since we have candidate models that vary in discrimination, certain multilevel modeling packages cannot be used, notably lme4. However, structural equation modeling packages that can deal with ordinal outcomes can be used. They have the advantage of allowing more flexibility in structure, but it is not always easy to impose constraints on category structures or to compute item category response functions, reliability, and other pieces of information. In this context, IRT software capable of fitting ordinal models would be ideal. For the rest of this example, I used jrt (Myszkowski, 2021), which provides convenience functions for IRT models that involve multiple judges and uses as its estimation package mirt (Chalmers, 2012).

4.2.5 Application

All models were successfully estimated. Using likelihood ratio tests, we find that the rating scale model is significantly outperformed in fit by the partial credit model, and the partial credit model is significantly outperformed by the generalized partial credit model (this is not surprising, since it is the model used to generate the data). The AIC also suggests that the generalized partial credit model fits best. Based on the combination of these results, we conclude that the generalized partial credit model is, overall, the best-fitting model.

4.2.6 Benefits of IRT

Compared with a CTT approach, which would generally imply using a combination of sum/average scoring and Cronbach's α (or ICC) (Myszkowski & Storme, 2019), the approach used has multiple advantages.

First, we know that finding and/or compensating expert judges can be demanding of resources. While solutions to this can involve using layperson judgments (Hass, Rivera, & Silvia, 2018), training them (Storme, Myszkowski, Çelic, et al., 2014), or using semantic analysis (Beaty & Johnson, 2020), another approach is to use a planned missingness judgment design, similar to the one we used here. Not all judges assess the same products, which is less demanding.

Second, many tools for measuring reliability have been developed over the years, particularly for inter-rater reliability (Cseh & Jeffries, 2019). In this example, many of these tools are simply not available for missing data. Further, even if we use plausible value imputation, their range can be dramatic – in this example, we found, for example, a Fleiss's κ of 0.26, a Cronbach's α of 0.81, and ICCs of around 0.53. In this context, how is one to decide whether the reliability is sufficient or compute standard errors of measurement (or confidence intervals) that are meaningful? The answer – at least the one I recommend – is to use a measure of reliability that is based on a sound measurement model that has been tested on the data. Here, using our best-fitting model, an empirical reliability of 0.66 is observed in the sample and a reliability of 0.71 is expected in the population (assuming a standard normal distribution of θ). A more model-agnostic alternative is to use a model-averaged reliability estimate.

Finally, like in the previous example, we may question the benefits of IRT by judging its accuracy relative to CTT scoring (i.e., using averages). One difference from our previous example is that this time the data has been simulated, and therefore the true θ values are known. Thus we can compare the model estimates $\hat{\theta}$s with the true θs and see whether a better estimation is obtained with IRT modeling instead of average scoring (with z-transformation). We found in our example data that the root mean squared difference between estimates and true θ values (RMSE) was substantially improved from 1.07 using average and standardized scores to 0.55. The mean absolute error (MAE) dropped from 0.91 to 0.42.

To note here, RMSE and MAE values can be interpreted as measures of the typical distance between predictions and true θ values, which were drawn from a standard Gaussian distribution. Thus the difference observed can be interpreted as about half a standard deviation. A graphical comparison of the distribution of the differences between estimates and true values is shown in Figure 33. Of course, the following result should still be thought of as an example, as it is dependent upon the number of response categories, the data generation model, the sample size, and the planned missingness design.

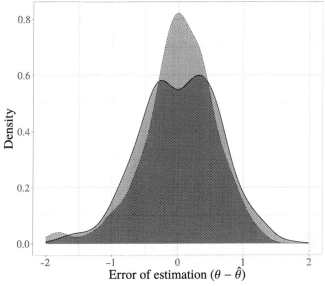

Figure 33 Differences between true θs and estimates from average scoring (plain line) vs. IRT factor scoring (dashed line)

5 Future Uses of IRT in Creativity Research

In this section, I aim to discuss extensions and advanced uses of IRT that could substantially improve the way we research creativity and the way that creativity can be efficiently and accurately measured.

Before I discuss potential future directions, it is important to acknowledge that IRT, although uncommon, has been used in creativity research. Binary logistic IRT models have, for example, been used to study a number of tests used in creativity research, including the remote associates test (e.g., Akbari Chermahini, Hickendorff, & Hommel, 2012; Salvi, Costantini, Pace, et al., 2020) and the visual aesthetic sensitivity test (Myszkowski & Storme, 2017). Forthmann, Paek, Dumas, et al. (2020) also present how to use logistic models in the measurement of originality in divergent thinking tasks. Further, models for count data have been used in the context of divergent thinking fluency scores (Baghaei & Doebler, 2019; Myszkowski & Storme, 2021), and log-linear response models have been used to model response times to the visual aesthetic sensitivity test (Myszkowski, 2019). We shall also note that various models for ordinal data, including many-facets models, have been used to model creativity ratings (Barbot, Kaufman, & Myszkowski, 2023; Myszkowski, 2021; Myszkowski & Storme, 2019; Primi, Silvia, Jauk, et al., 2019; Tan, Mourges, Hein, et al., 2015). Finally, we shall note that if one considers traditional factor models to be subsumed into IRT (Mellenbergh,

1994), as in this Element, we should consider as uses of IRT the numerous uses of linear measurement models in creativity research (e.g., Barbot, Besançon, & Lubart, 2016; Kaufman, 2012; Silvia, Beaty, & Nusbaum, 2013; Storme, Lubart, Myszkowski, et al., 2017).

5.1 Maximizing the Efficiency of the Consensual Assessment Technique

Measurements that specifically gain from more advanced statistical models are often those that have stringent constraints. As noted previously, an important constraint in creativity research is reliance on human judgments to judge creative products on various criteria.

Such a measurement paradigm is particularly consuming in terms of resources, because a judge is a person and not an item, which implies a cost (in time, organization, compensation, expertise, etc.) relative to each judgment. As we mentioned, leveraging computational approaches is a promising route to limit – and eventually suppress – rating costs, but it is still unclear whether these new approaches will be applicable, accurate, and accepted in all creativity domains. In a context without a lot of alternatives, IRT presents several advantages that I believe are still underused. In general, these advantages all aim to reduce the number of judgments necessary for the estimation of the construct studied.

5.2 Planned Missingness in the Calibration Data

Item-response theory permits us to minimize the number of judges necessary to achieve accurate measurement. As we suggest through our example, it is possible to create designs where not all judges rate the products of all persons. Item-response theory deals with such situations by allowing the estimation of person and item parameters even in the presence of missing data. The missing data leads to a loss of information/reliability, of course, but such loss is quantifiable and thus can be anticipated. In contrast, CTT-based measures of reliability can provide reliability with or without a judge/item completely – not just without a judge/item judging a particular product. I believe that researchers should consider more often the use of IRT with planned missingness designs (see for an introduction Kolen & Brennan, 2014). Because the presence of anchor judges allows simultaneous model estimations, common-item (here judge) random group designs (such as the design presented in the examples section) are in my opinion particularly practical. For this to be considered more often, simulation studies in the field of creativity would be prescribed, as they could more clearly discuss benefits and risks (e.g., nonconvergence) and provide guidelines (or at least rules of thumb) for which missing data plan to adopt given a particular situation.

5.3 Computerized Adaptive Judgment

Another use of the capabilities of IRT for missing data is computerized adaptive testing (Weiss, 1982). With computerized adaptive testing, it is possible to reduce the number of presented items to a given person by estimating and reestimating after each item that person's latent level and subsequently presenting items that are expected to provide the most information. Past a degree of information/reliability achieved (or a number of items taken, or some other constraint), the test can be stopped without the person taking all items. The procedure of adaptive testing, although typically applied to item presentation, could be adapted to the presentation of products to judges. That is, we could imagine that judges would be requested to rate a product only on the condition that it would provide substantial information on the (currently estimated) creativity of the product.

Of course, this probably seems like a stretch of the imagination for a small study because we picture raters receiving products to judge one at a time, which does not seem very practical. Still, for a larger-scale study, we could imagine judges receiving assignments in batches, each batch of products being assembled based on the results of the previous batches. In other words, each judge would receive products to judge that match the level at which their expertise has the most value. Of course, more work is needed to determine under which conditions computerized adaptive judgment is reasonably feasible and beneficial.

5.4 Optimal Judge Panel Designs

Finally, provided that a large enough pool of judges is obtained and that their characteristics (i.e., severity, discrimination, etc.) are estimated in an IRT framework, it is then possible to assemble an optimal set (or parallel sets) of judges for a product or set of products. The framework of *optimal test design* (OTD; van der Linden, 2005) – or optimal test assembly – discusses how to select items (here judges) in order to optimize the qualities of an instrument (e.g., the amount of expected total information provided by the test, assuming a distribution of examinees) while satisfying various constraints (e.g., number of items/judges, item/judge exposure). In the context of the consensual assessment technique, an *optimal judge panel design* could be constructed, allowing us to improve – in reliability and perhaps in validity and fairness – the way we put together judge panels.

5.5 Using Collateral Information

One exciting development of IRT is its capacity to account for various phenomena related to the measurement situation over and beyond the item responses themselves. Notably, thanks to computerized testing and online survey methods, it has become increasingly easy to obtain information collateral to testing, such as the number of response changes or the response times. Studies using joint response times and response models have recently been particularly discussed (Fox, Klein Entink, & van der Linden, 2007; Fox & Marianti, 2016; Goldhammer & Klein Entink, 2011; Klein Entink, Kuhn, Hornke, et al., 2009; Marianti, Fox, Avetisyan, et al., 2014; Myszkowski, 2019; Myszkowski, Storme, Kubiak, et al., 2022; Shaw, Elizondo, & Wadlington, 2020; van der Linden, Klein Entink, & Fox, 2010). They have allowed us to uncover interesting phenomena, such as a speed–accuracy trade-off in cognitive tests at the between-individual level, even in nonspeeded tests.

In the context of creativity research, I believe that this methodology is particularly promising and would have multiple applications. First, response times, once modeled, can be flagged as statistically improbable for a given person and item (e.g., an item usually rapidly responded to and responded to by a person who responds fast has a short expected time response). Thus we could imagine building an outlier detection method based on these models in order to detect potentially aberrant responses.

This could be applied, for example, to detect judgments of creative products that have been made too hastily by a judge – possibly leading to discarding the judgment and/or having the judge (or another judge) rate the product again. Further studies should investigate how this might be feasible in various contexts and the potential benefits. I would speculate that modeling response times this way is particularly pertinent for judgments of written productions (e.g., essays, stories, descriptions, etc.), because the reading time involved in judgment would probably make the overall judgment times particularly predictable with a response time model. Apart from detecting hasty judgments, the study of judgment time could help us to better understand how creativity judgment speed relates to various factors (e.g., judgment accuracy, judge expertise, judgment fatigue, judge personality traits, incentives).

Beyond rater-mediated measures, IRT response time models could also be used in studying various other creativity measures. For example, it could help us understand the flow of producing responses in divergent thinking tasks or detect social desirability effects (i.e., faking) in creativity self-report measures.

Finally, it is likely that other forms of collateral information will appear in the future. For example, it is possible that eye-tracking technology will eventually be easily and inexpensively embedded in webcams and front cameras and that survey software will easily integrate it, providing yet another stream of incoming data to analyze. This could provide ways to better measure attention and its fluctuations during a test (or a judgment of products), further helping us to estimate and understand constructs.

5.6 Connecting Item Response Theory with Formative Models

Recently, psychometric research has extensively debated reflective measurement (which is common to IRT and CTT), along with local independence. The assumption has been challenged conceptually by the idea that constructs could be formed from item responses instead (Bollen & Lennox, 1991). This approach is often referred to as *formative measurement* or as domain behavior theory (see Bollen & Diamantopoulos, 2017, for a defense and discussion of methods related to that approach). In formative models, items are not caused by a construct and they are allowed to covary with one another – hence local dependencies are allowed.

Formative approaches, when considered for an instrument, are generally thought to be appropriate when items are built from a sampling process of domains of behavior. The latent variable, in this approach, is essentially a weighted average of the sampled domains, which the researcher assumes pertinent. Borsboom, Mellenbergh, and van Heerden (2003) give the example of regrouping income, educational level, and neighborhood into a single latent variable to represent socio-economic status.

In creativity research, it is in fact frequent to build measures that sample from different domains and to then want to regroup them under the umbrella term of creativity – although that is not always represented in the model – without necessarily much conviction that a common factor of creativity caused them. In this context, formative models may be useful to regroup domains together into a single entity (e.g., creativity), notably in order to predict other variables. For example, if we are using the Kaufman Domains of Creativity Scale (K-DOCS; Kaufman, 2012), where five domains of creativity are measured by multiple items, to predict a number of outcomes (e.g., satisfaction with life and sense of meaning), we could imagine a model where the five domains are measured with a reflective model (each domain causes its item responses), while the domain variables would themselves form a cross-domain creativity factor (the term *general creativity* might not be appropriate, since it is seen as dependent upon which domains were measured and also dependent upon what outcomes are predicted). This creativity factor would then be estimated as explanatory

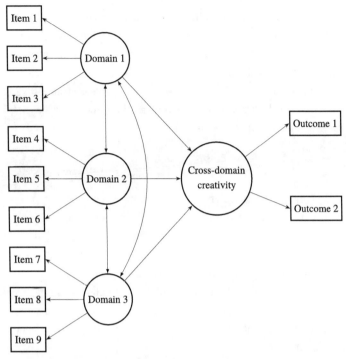

Figure 34 Conceptual representation of a hybrid reflective–formative model, with reflective domains and a formative cross-domain creativity factor used to explain outcome variables

of satisfaction with life and sense of meaning. In sum, we would have here an IRT model at the item level and a formative model at the domain level, forming a predictor for a structural (regression) model. Such an approach is interesting in that (1) domains are more accurately measured as latent variables than they would be as sum scores (i.e., some measurement errors are controlled for), (2) the domains are used to form a creativity variable without assuming it to be the cause of the domains (i.e., we do not assume domain generality), and (3) the domains are weighted in order to most accurately predict a set of outcomes, therefore this model could be used to study the relative contributions of domains. I show this structural model in a path diagram in Figure 34. Since we are often dealing with domain specificity in creativity, we are also often dealing with domain sampling, and hybrid approaches like this may be promising.

5.7 Connecting Item Response Theory with Network Models

Network psychometric models represent one of the most discussed developments in the field of psychometrics. They are a radical alternative to reflective models, and thus to IRT, in that, in network models, item responses directly covary (i.e., they are locally dependent) but are not explained by a latent variable (Borsboom & Cramer, 2013). In other words, such models imply that the constructs are best understood as sets of behaviors (measured with items) that directly influence one another. This conceptual approach is sometimes referred to as a *mutualist* approach (as opposed to a reflective approach).

In a number of situations and in various fields, network models have been discussed as realistic explanations for the interrelations between item responses (i.e., positive manifold situations) (e.g., Myszkowski, Storme, & Çelik, 2023; van der Maas, Dolan, Grasman, et al., 2006). A key advantage of this new approach is that it does not require us to assume the existence of a latent variable and still achieves a number of important objectives usually aimed at in psychometrics – such as identifying facets, identifying redundant items, and producing an estimation for person attributes (Christensen & Golino, 2021; Christensen, Golino, & Silvia, 2020; Golino, Christensen, Garrido, et al., 2020). In a few words, network psychometric analysis generally consists of using various methods (e.g., EBICglasso) to prune local dependencies between items in order to reduce them to a sparse, parsimonious, and reproducible set of relations – the network model – and then using a number of graphical methods (e.g., node distance measures, centrality indices, cluster identification algorithms) to obtain various information about the model (Costantini, Epskamp, Borsboom, et al., 2015).

Assuming latent variables cause locally independent item responses is central in IRT, and the opposite is certainly central in network psychometrics. But it does not mean that the two approaches are completely incompatible. Notably, new modeling approaches allow hybrids between reflective models and network models (Kan, de Jonge, van der Maas, et al., 2020), with for example, latent network models, which consist of latent variables estimated reflectively, while their interrelations are determined through network modeling methods. It is also possible to build residual network models, where the item responses are caused by a (set of) latent variable(s), while their residuals are not all locally independent and where the local dependencies are conceptualized and estimated as a network. Latent variable models with networks modeling both the local dependencies and the relations between latents are also possible. These hybrid models are largely developed for variance–covariance structures, so they are, for now at least, combinations of network models with (linear) structural equation models more than item response theory models. Nevertheless, it appears possible to imagine the development of such hybrid reflective-network models where the reflective part is based on item response theory modeling.

In my opinion, there are many possible applications of such hybrids for creativity research. For example, they could be used as an approach to the question of domain generality in creativity, as it could allow the consideration of a general creativity factor (i.e., reflective model) – or perhaps several interconnected large creative domains – while the domains could have direct interconnections (i.e., local dependencies) unknown a priori (and possibly best studied through a network approach).

Further, on a less conceptual level, it is possible that many instruments used and developed in our field are better understood with such approaches. For example, in measures employing the consensual assessment technique, it is possible that the assumption of local independence does not hold regarding judges, as panels of judges may include clusters of judges that come from similar backgrounds (e.g., same degree) or have the same occupation or who actually even know one another. In this context, a residual network model could be appropriate to allow the identification and modeling of such local dependencies.

6 Conclusion

Classical test theory provides a set of tools that are easy to use and available in many software packages. These tools – the most prominent being sum/average scoring and Cronbach's α, along with subsequent techniques, such as the standard errors of measurement and confidence intervals computed from α – have certainly become go-to procedures for many researchers and test developers. Yet in spite of their practicality and them being sufficiently accurate in some cases, I hope to have demonstrated that CTT has important shortcomings for creativity researchers.

In this Element, I do not suggest that researchers abandon CTT models, sum scoring, or Cronbach's α. However, I suggest they consider its multiple assumptions (linear response functions, Gaussian item distributions, etc.) in any context that requires psychological measurement. In other words, I recommend abandoning the axiomatic use of CTT while retaining its statistical models. Seeing CTT as a class of statistical models and a subset of IRT models does not dismiss CTT models as being insufficiently accurate or not conceptually sound, but it implies that the assumptions of such models can – and need to – be discussed and challenged, theoretically and empirically. Further, it implies that estimating person attributes (i.e., achieving measurement) needs to come as a consequence of accurately describing item data with a statistical model.

Even when seen as a subset of IRT, CTT models still present a number of issues for the measurement of psychological attributes, and this is particularly true in the field of creativity. IRT can be described as a general statistical modeling approach to the estimation of individual attributes (i.e., constructs) from the observation of behaviors. Such a broad approach opens many doors: it allows and accounts for nonlinear response models, non-Gaussian measurement errors, multidimensionality, hybrid response models, heterogeneous examinee populations, and missing data, among many other things. Further, by separating scores from person (and item) attributes, IRT prevents a number of conceptual confusions.

Certainly, IRT remains a minority approach and requires thinking more carefully about measurement than we are used to, but it comes with the reward of models that are often more empirically accurate and conceptually reasonable. In my view, IRT respects the complexity of psychological measurement, while (the usual axiomatic view of) CTT dismisses it. Creativity researchers are usually so resourceful when it comes to inventing new and original measurement paradigms (e.g., Barron & Welsh, 1952) that they might have made it an art form, yet they lack interest in describing the underlying probabilistic mechanisms of these measurements – which, perhaps, is also a creative act (Myszkowski, 2020; Thissen, 2001).

This Element is intended to serve as an introduction – not as a manifesto. Nevertheless, I do believe that creativity measurement presents numerous exciting challenges that IRT could accurately and elegantly address. I hope that this overview of such a cryptic framework will spike curiosity, and I believe that it can serve as entry point to test theory – classical and modern – for many current and future creativity researchers. I suppose this is the first book to discuss IRT in the field of creativity, but I do not expect it to be the last.

References

Akbari Chermahini, S., Hickendorff, M., & Hommel, B. (2012). Development and validity of a Dutch version of the remote associates task: An item-response theory approach. *Thinking Skills and Creativity*, *7*(3), 177–186. DOI: https://10.1016/j.tsc.2012.02.003

Albert, J. H. (2017). Logit, probit, and other response functions. In W. J. van der Linden (ed.), *Handbook of item response theory, Volume 2: Statistical tools* (pp. 3–22). Chapman and Hall/CRC.

Amabile, T. M. (1982). Social psychology of creativity: A consensual assessment technique. *Journal of Personality and Social Psychology*, *43*(5), 997–1013. DOI: https://10.1037/0022-3514.43.5.997

Andrich, D. (1978). A rating formulation for ordered response categories. *Psychometrika*, *43*(4), 561–573. DOI: https://10.1007/BF02293814

Baer, J. (2012). Domain specificity and the limits of creativity theory. *Journal of Creative Behavior*, *46*(1), 16–29. DOI: https://10.1002/jocb.002

Baghaei, P., & Doebler, P. (2019). Introduction to the Rasch Poisson counts model: An R tutorial. *Psychological Reports*, *122*(5), 1967–1994. DOI: https://10.1177/0033294118797577

Barbot, B., Besançon, M., & Lubart, T. (2016). The generality-specificity of creativity: Exploring the structure of creative potential with EPoC. *Learning and Individual Differences*, *52*, 178–187. DOI: https://10.1016/j.lindif.2016.06.005

Barbot, B., Kaufman, J. C., & Myszkowski, N. (2023). Creativity with 6 degrees of freedom: Feasibility study of visual creativity assessment in virtual reality. *Creativity Research Journal*, *35*(4), 783–800. DOI: https://10.1080/10400419.2023.2193040

Barron, F., & Welsh, G. S. (1952). Artistic perception as a possible factor in personality style: Its measurement by a figure preference test. *Journal of Psychology*, *33*(2), 199–203. DOI: https://10.1080/00223980.1952.9712830

Bates, D., Mächler, M., Bolker, B., et al (2015). Fitting linear mixed-effects models using lme4. *Journal of Statistical Software*, *67*(1), 1–48. DOI: https://10.18637/jss.v067.i01

Batey, M. (2012). The measurement of creativity: From definitional consensus to the introduction of a new heuristic framework. *Creativity Research Journal, 24*(1), 55–65. DOI: https://10.1080/10400419.2012.649181

Beaty, R. E., & Johnson, D. R. (2020). Automating creativity assessment with SemDis: An open platform for computing semantic distance. *Behavior Research Methods*. DOI: https://10.3758/s13428-020-01453-w

Besemer, S. P. (1998). Creative product analysis matrix: Testing the model structure and a comparison among products – three novel chairs. *Creativity Research Journal, 11*(4), 333–346. DOI: https://10.1207/s15326934 crj1104_7

Birnbaum, A., Lord, F. M., & Novick, M. R. (1968). Some latent trait models and their use in inferring an examinee's ability. In *Statistical theories of mental test scores* (pp. 397–472). Reading, MA: Addison Wesley.

Bock, R. D. (1972). Estimating item parameters and latent ability when responses are scored in two or more nominal categories. *Psychometrika, 37*(1), 29–51. DOI: https://10.1007/BF02291411

Bock, R. D., & Aitkin, M. (1982). Marginal maximum likelihood estimation of item parameters: Application of an EM algorithm. *Psychometrika, 46*(4), 443–459. DOI: https://10.1007/BF02294168

Bock, R. D., Gibbons, R., & Muraki, E. (1988). Full-information item factor analysis. *Applied Psychological Measurement, 12*(3), 261–280. DOI: https://10.1177/014662168801200305

Boeck, P. D., Bakker, M., Zwitser, R., et al. (2011). The estimation of item response models with the lmer function from the lme4 package in R. *Journal of Statistical Software, 39*(12), 1–28. DOI: https://10.18637/jss.v039.i12

Bollen, K., & Diamantopoulos, A. (2017). In defense of causal-formative indicators: A minority report. *Psychological Methods, 22*(3), 581–596. DOI: https://10.1037/met0000056

Bollen, K., & Lennox, R. (1991). Conventional wisdom on measurement: A structural equation perspective. *Psychological Bulletin, 110*(2), 305–314. DOI: https://10.1037/0033-2909.110.2.305

Bonifay, W. E., Reise, S. P., Scheines, R., et al. (2015). When are multidimensional data unidimensional enough for structural equation modeling? An evaluation of the DETECT multidimensionality index. *Structural Equation Modeling: A Multidisciplinary Journal, 22*(4), 504–516. DOI: https://10.1080/10705511.2014.938596

Borsboom, D. (2006). The attack of the psychometricians. *Psychometrika, 71*(3), 425–440. DOI: https://10.1007/s11336-006-1447-6

Borsboom, D., & Cramer, A. O. (2013). Network analysis: An integrative approach to the structure of psychopathology. *Annual Review of Clinical*

Psychology, *9*(1), 91–121. DOI: https://10.1146/annurev-clinpsy-050212-185608

Borsboom, D., & Mellenbergh, G. J. (2002). True scores, latent variables, and constructs: A comment on Schmidt and Hunter. *Intelligence, 30*(6), 505–514. DOI: https://10.1016/S0160-2896(02)00082-X

Borsboom, D., Mellenbergh, G. J., & van Heerden, J. (2003). The theoretical status of latent variables. *Psychological Review, 110*(2), 203–219. DOI: https://10.1037/0033-295X.110.2.203

Bürkner, P.- C. (2017). Brms: An R package for Bayesian multilevel models using Stan. *Journal of Statistical Software, 80*(1), 1–28. DOI: https://10.18637/jss.v080.i01

Bürkner, P.- C. (2020). Analysing standard progressive matrices (spm-ls) with Bayesian item response models. *Journal of Intelligence, 8*(1), 1–18. DOI: https://10.3390/jintelligence8010005

Cai, L., & Hansen, M. (2013). Limited-information goodness-of-fit testing of hierarchical item factor models. *British Journal of Mathematical and Statistical Psychology, 66*(2), 245–276. DOI: https://10.1111/j.2044-8317.2012.02050.x

Chalmers, R. P. (2012). Mirt: A multidimensional item response theory package for the R environment. *Journal of Statistical Software, 48*(1), 1–29. DOI: https://10.18637/jss.v048.i06

Chen, W.- H., & Thissen, D. (1997). Local dependence indexes for item pairs using item response theory. *Journal of Educational and Behavioral Statistics, 22*(3), 265–289. DOI: https://10.2307/1165285

Christensen, A. P., & Golino, H. F. (2021). On the equivalency of factor and network loadings. *Behavior Research Methods, 53*(4), 1563–1580. DOI: https://10.3758/s13428-020-01500-6

Christensen, A. P., Golino, H. F., & Silvia, P. J. (2020). A psychometric network perspective on the validity and validation of personality trait questionnaires. *European Journal of Personality, 34*(6), 1095–1108. DOI: https://10.1002/per.2265

Costantini, G., Epskamp, S., Borsboom, D., et al. (2015). State of the aRt personality research: A tutorial on network analysis of personality data in R. *Journal of Research in Personality, 54*(Supplement C), 13–29. DOI: https://10.1016/j.jrp.2014.07.003

Cseh, G. M., & Jeffries, K. K. (2019). A scattered CAT: A critical evaluation of the consensual assessment technique for creativity research. *Psychology of Aesthetics, Creativity, and the Arts, 13*(2), 159–166. DOI: https://10.1037/aca0000220

De Ayala, R. J. (2022). *The theory and practice of item response theory* (2nd ed.). New York: Guilford Press.

De Boeck, P. (2008). Random item IRT models. *Psychometrika, 73*(4), 533–559. DOI: https://10.1007/s11336-008-9092-x

De Boeck, P. (2011). *Explanatory item response models: A generalized linear and nonlinear approach*. New York: Springer.

Doebler, A., Doebler, P., & Holling, H. (2014). A latent ability model for count data and application to processing speed. *Applied Psychological Measurement, 38*(8), 587–598. DOI: https://10.1177/0146621614543513

Drasgow, F., Levine, M. V., & McLaughlin, M. E. (1987). Detecting inappropriate test scores with optimal and practical appropriateness indices. *Applied Psychological Measurement, 11*(1), 59–79. DOI: https://10.1177/014662168701100105

Embretson, S. E., & Reise, S. P. (2000). *Item response theory for psychologists* (1st ed.). Mahwah, NJ: Psychology Press.

Fischer, G. H. (1973). The linear logistic test model as an instrument in educational research. *Acta Psychologica, 37*(6), 359–374. DOI: https://10.1016/0001-6918(73)90003-6

Forthmann, B., & Doebler, P. (2021). Reliability of researcher capacity estimates and count data dispersion: A comparison of Poisson, negative binomial, and Conway-Maxwell Poisson models. *Scientometrics, 126*, 3337–3354. DOI: https://10.1007/s11192-021-03864-8

Forthmann, B., Paek, S. H., Dumas, D., et al. (2020). Scrutinizing the basis of originality in divergent thinking tests: On the measurement precision of response propensity estimates. *British Journal of Educational Psychology, 90*(3), 683–699. DOI: https://10.1111/bjep.12325

Fox, J.- P., Klein Entink, R. H., & van der Linden, W. J. (2007). Modeling of responses and response times with the CIRT package. *Journal of Statistical Software, 20*(7), 1–14. DOI: https://10.18637/jss.v020.i07

Fox, J.- P., & Marianti, S. (2016). Joint modeling of ability and differential speed using responses and response times. *Multivariate Behavioral Research, 51*(4), 540–553. DOI: https://10.1080/00273171.2016.1171128

Goldhammer, F., & Klein Entink, R. H. (2011). Speed of reasoning and its relation to reasoning ability. *Intelligence, 39*(2), 108–119. DOI: https://10.1016/j.intell.2011.02.001

Golino, H. F., Shi, D., Christensen, A. P., et al. (2020). Investigating the performance of exploratory graph analysis and traditional techniques to identify the number of latent factors: A simulation and tutorial. *Psychological Methods, 25*(3), 292–320. DOI: https://10.1037/met0000255

Graham, J. M. (2006). Congeneric and (essentially) tau-equivalent estimates of score reliability: What they are and how to use them. *Educational and Psychological Measurement, 66*(6), 930–944. DOI: https://10.1177/0013164406288165

Hass, R. W., Rivera, M., & Silvia, P. J. (2018). On the dependability and feasibility of layperson ratings of divergent thinking. *Frontiers in Psychology, 9*, 1–13. DOI: https://10.3389/fpsyg.2018.01343

Hohle, R. H. (1965). Inferred components of reaction times as functions of foreperiod duration. *Journal of Experimental Psychology, 69*(4), 382–386. DOI: https://10.1037/h0021740

Hu, L., & Bentler, P. M. (1999). Cutoff criteria for fit indexes in covariance structure analysis: Conventional criteria versus new alternatives. *Structural Equation Modeling: A Multidisciplinary Journal, 6*(1), 1–55. DOI: https://10.1080/10705519909540118

Hung, L.- F. (2012). A negative binomial regression model for accuracy tests. *Applied Psychological Measurement, 36*(2), 88–103. DOI: https://10.1177/0146621611429548

Kan, K.- J., de Jonge, H., van der Maas, H. L. J., et al. (2020). How to compare psychometric factor and network models. *Journal of Intelligence, 8*(4), 1–10. DOI: https://10.3390/jintelligence8040035

Kaufman, J. C. (2012). Counting the muses: Development of the Kaufman domains of creativity scale (K-DOCS). *Psychology of Aesthetics, Creativity, and the Arts, 6*(4), 298–308. DOI: https://10.1037/a0029751

Kaufman, J. C., Baer, J., & Cole, J. C. (2009). Expertise, domains, and the consensual assessment technique. *Journal of Creative Behavior, 43*(4), 223–233. DOI: https://10.1002/j.2162-6057.2009.tb01316.x

Kaufman, J. C., & Beghetto, R. A. (2009). Beyond big and little: The four C model of creativity. *Review of General Psychology, 13*(1), 1–12. DOI: https://10.1037/a0013688

Klein Entink, R. H., Kuhn, J.- T., Hornke, L. F., et al. (2009). Evaluating cognitive theory: A joint modeling approach using responses and response times. *Psychological Methods, 14*(1), 54–75. DOI: https://10.1037/a0014877

Kolen, M. J., & Brennan, R. L. (2014). *Test equating, scaling, and linking: Methods and practices.* New York, NY: Springer. DOI: https://10.1007/978-1-4939-0317-7

Lord, F. M. (1951). A theory of test scores and their relation to the trait measured. *ETS Research Bulletin Series, 1951*(1), i–126. DOI: https://10.1002/j.2333-8504.1951.tb00922.x

Lord, F. M., & Novick, M. R. (2008). *Statistical theories of mental test scores.* Charlotte: Information Age Publishing.

Lumsden, J. (1976). Test theory. *Annual Review of Psychology, 27*(1), 251–280. DOI: https://10.1146/annurev.ps.27.020176.001343

Mair, P., & Hatzinger, R. (2007). Extended Rasch modeling: The eRm package for the application of IRT models in R. *Journal of Statistical Software, 20*(9), 1–20. DOI: https://10.18637/jss.v020.i09

Marianti, S., Fox, J.- P., Avetisyan, M., et al. (2014). Testing for aberrant behavior in response time modeling. *Journal of Educational and Behavioral Statistics, 39*(6), 426–451. DOI: https://10.3102/1076998614559412

Masters, G. N. (1982). A Rasch model for partial credit scoring. *Psychometrika, 47*(2), 149–174. DOI: https://10.1007/BF02296272

Maydeu-Olivares, A. (2013). Goodness-of-fit assessment of item response theory models. *Measurement: Interdisciplinary Research and Perspectives, 11*(3), 71–101. DOI: https://10.1080/15366367.2013.831680

Maydeu-Olivares, A., & Joe, H. (2006). Limited information goodness-of-fit testing in multidimensional contingency tables. *Psychometrika, 71*(4), 713–732. DOI: https://10.1007/s11336-005-1295-9

McKinley, R. L., & Mills, C. N. (1985). A comparison of several goodness-of-fit statistics. *Applied Psychological Measurement, 9*(1), 49–57. DOI: https://10.1177/014662168500900105

McNeish, D., & Wolf, M. G. (2020). Thinking twice about sum scores. *Behavior Research Methods, 52*(6), 2287–2305. DOI: https://10.3758/s13428-020-01398-0

Mellenbergh, G. J. (1994). Generalized linear item response theory. *Psychological Bulletin, 115*(2), 300–307. DOI: https://10.1037/0033-2909.115.2.300

Muraki, E. (1990). Fitting a polytomous item response model to Likert-type data. *Applied Psychological Measurement, 14*(1), 59–71. DOI: https://10.1177/014662169001400106

Muraki, E. (1992). A generalized partial credit model: Application of an EM algorithm. *ETS Research Report Series, 1992*(1), 1–30. DOI: https://10.1002/j.2333-8504.1992.tb01436.x

Muraki, E. (1997). A generalized partial credit model. In W. J. van der Linden & R. K. Hambleton (eds.), *Handbook of modern item response theory* (pp. 153–164). New York, NY: Springer. DOI: https://10.1007/978-1-4757-2691-6_9

Myszkowski, N. (2019). The first glance is the weakest: "Tasteful" individuals are slower to judge visual art. *Personality and Individual Differences, 141*, 188–195. DOI: https://10.1016/j.paid.2019.01.010

Myszkowski, N. (2020). Analysis of an intelligence dataset. *Journal of Intelligence, 8*(4), 1–3. DOI: https://10.3390/jintelligence8040039

Myszkowski, N. (2021). Development of the R library "jrt": Automated item response theory procedures for judgment data and their application with the consensual assessment technique. *Psychology of Aesthetics, Creativity, and the Arts*, *15*(3), 426–438. DOI: https://10.1037/aca0000287

Myszkowski, N., Barbot, B., & Zenasni, F. (2022). Cognitive and conative profiles of creative people. In T. Lubart, M. Botella, S. Bourgeois-Bougrine, et al. (eds.), *Homo creativus: The 7 C's of human creativity* (pp. 33–48). Cham: Springer. DOI: https://10.1007/978-3-030-99674-1_3

Myszkowski, N., & Storme, M. (2017). Measuring "good taste" with the visual aesthetic sensitivity test-revised (VAST-R). *Personality and Individual Differences*, *117*, 91–100. DOI: https://10.1016/j.paid.2017.05.041

Myszkowski, N., & Storme, M. (2018). A snapshot of g? Binary and polytomous item-response theory investigations of the last series of the standard progressive matrices (SPM-LS). *Intelligence*, *68*, 109–116. DOI: https://10.1016/j.intell.2018.03.010

Myszkowski, N., & Storme, M. (2019). Judge response theory? A call to upgrade our psychometrical account of creativity judgments. *Psychology of Aesthetics, Creativity, and the Arts*, *13*(2), 167–175. DOI: https://10.1037/aca0000225

Myszkowski, N., & Storme, M. (2021). Accounting for variable task discrimination in divergent thinking fluency measurement: An example of the benefits of a 2-parameter Poisson counts model and its bifactor extension over the Rasch Poisson counts model. *Journal of Creative Behavior*, *55*(3), 800–818. DOI: https://10.1002/jocb.490

Myszkowski, N., Storme, M., Kubiak, E., et al. (2022). Exploring the associations between personality and response speed trajectories in low-stakes intelligence tests. *Personality and Individual Differences*, *191*(111580), 1–9. DOI: https://10.1016/j.paid.2022.111580

Myszkowski, N., Storme, M., & Çelik, P. (2023). One common factor, four resources, both, or neither: A network model of career adaptability resources. *Measurement and Evaluation in Counseling and Development*, *56*(3), 209–224. DOI: https://10.1080/07481756.2022.2073894

Nicewander, W. A. (2018). Conditional reliability coefficients for test scores. *Psychological Methods 23*(2), 351–362. DOI: https://10.1037/met0000132

Noel, Y., & Dauvier, B. (2007). A beta item response model for continuous bounded responses. *Applied Psychological Measurement*, *31*(1), 47–73. DOI: https://10.1177/0146621605287691

Novick, M. R. (1966). The axioms and principal results of classical test theory. *Journal of Mathematical Psychology*, *3*(1), 1–18. DOI: https://10.1016/0022-2496(66)90002-2

Orlando, M., & Thissen, D. (2000). Likelihood-based item-fit indices for dichotomous item response theory models. *Applied Psychological Measurement, 24*(1), 50–64. DOI: https://10.1177/01466216000241003

Ostini, R., & Nering, M. (2006). *Polytomous item response theory models.* Thousand Oaks, CA: SAGE. DOI: https://10.4135/9781412985413

Palmer, E. M., Horowitz, T. S., Torralba, A., et al. (2011). What are the shapes of response time distributions in visual search? *Journal of Experimental Psychology: Human Perception and Performance, 37*(1), 58–71. DOI: https://10.1037/a0020747

Patz, R. J., Junker, B. W., Johnson, M. S., et al. (2002). The hierarchical rater model for rated test items and its application to large-scale educational assessment data. *Journal of Educational and Behavioral Statistics, 27*(4), 341–384. DOI: https://10.3102/10769986027004341

Primi, R., Silvia, P. J., Jauk, E., et al. (2019). Applying many-facet Rasch modeling in the assessment of creativity. *Psychology of Aesthetics, Creativity, and the Arts, 13*(2), 176–186. DOI: https://10.1037/aca0000230

Qian, M., & Plucker, J. A. (2017). Creativity assessment. In J. Plucker (ed.), *Creativity and innovation.* (pp. 223–234) Waco: Routledge.

Raju, N. S., Price, L. R., Oshima, T., et al. (2007). Standardized conditional SEM: A case for conditional reliability. *Applied Psychological Measurement, 31*(3), 169–180. DOI: https://10.1177/0146621606291569

Rasch, G. (1960). *Studies in mathematical psychology: I. Probabilistic models for some intelligence and attainment tests.* Oxford: Nielsen & Lydiche.

Rhemtulla, M., Brosseau-Liard, P., & Savalei, V. (2012). When can categorical variables be treated as continuous? A comparison of robust continuous and categorical SEM estimation methods under suboptimal conditions. *Psychological Methods, 17*(3), 354–373. DOI: https://10.1037/a0029315

Rizopoulos, D. (2006). Ltm: An R package for latent variable modeling and item response analysis. *Journal of Statistical Software, 17*(5), 1–25. DOI: https://10.18637/jss.v017.i05

Robitzsch, A., & Steinfeld, J. (2018). Item response models for human ratings: Overview, estimation methods, and implementation in R. *Psychological Test and Assessment Modeling, 60*(1), 101–139.

Rosseel, Y. (2012). Lavaan: An R package for structural equation modeling. *Journal of Statistical Software, 48*(1), 1–36. DOI: http://10.18637/jss.v048.i02

Rost, J. (2001). The growing family of Rasch models. In A. Boomsma, M. A. J. van Duijn, & T. A. B. Snijders (eds.), *Essays on item response theory* (pp. 25–42). New York, NY: Springer. DOI: https://10.1007/978-1-4613-0169-1_2

Roussos, L. A., & Ozbek, O. Y. (2006). Formulation of the DETECT population parameter and evaluation of DETECT estimator bias. *Journal of Educational Measurement*, *43*(3), 215–243. DOI: https://doi.org/10.1111/j.1745-3984.2006.00014.x

Runco, M. A., & Jaeger, G. J. (2012). The standard definition of creativity. *Creativity Research Journal*, *24*(1), 92–96. DOI: https://10.1080/10400419.2012.650092

Salvi, C., Costantini, G., Pace, A., et al. (2020). Validation of the Italian remote associate test. *Journal of Creative Behavior*, *54*(1), 62–74. DOI: https://10.1002/jocb.345

Samejima, F. (1969). Estimation of latent ability using a response pattern of graded scores. *Psychometrika*, *34*(1), 1–97. DOI: https://10.1007/BF03372160

Schwarz, W. (2001). The ex-Wald distribution as a descriptive model of response times. *Behavior Research Methods, Instruments, & Computers*, *33*(4), 457–469. DOI: https://10.3758/BF03195403

Shaw, A., Elizondo, F., & Wadlington, P. L. (2020). Reasoning, fast and slow: How noncognitive factors may alter the ability-speed relationship. *Intelligence*, *83*, 101490. DOI: https://10.1016/j.intell.2020.101490

Sijtsma, K., & Junker, B. W. (1996). A survey of theory and methods of invariant item ordering. *British Journal of Mathematical and Statistical Psychology*, *49*(1), 79–105. DOI: https://10.1111/j.2044-8317.1996.tb01076.x

Sijtsma, K., & van der Ark, L. A. (2017). A tutorial on how to do a Mokken scale analysis on your test and questionnaire data. *British Journal of Mathematical and Statistical Psychology*, *70*(1), 137–158. DOI: https://10.1111/bmsp.12078

Silvia, P. J., Beaty, R. E., & Nusbaum, E. C. (2013). Verbal fluency and creativity: General and specific contributions of broad retrieval ability (Gr) factors to divergent thinking. *Intelligence*, *41*(5), 328–340. DOI: https://10.1016/j.intell.2013.05.004

Silvia, P. J., Winterstein, B. P., Willse, J. T., et al. (2008). Assessing creativity with divergent thinking tasks: Exploring the reliability and validity of new subjective scoring methods. *Psychology of Aesthetics, Creativity, and the Arts*, *2*(2), 68–85. DOI: https://10.1037/1931-3896.2.2.68

Snijders, T. A. B. (2001). Asymptotic null distribution of person fit statistics with estimated person parameter. *Psychometrika*, *66*(3), 331–342. DOI: https://10.1007/BF02294437

Storme, M., Lubart, T., Myszkowski, N., et al. (2017). A cross-cultural study of task specificity in creativity. *Journal of Creative Behavior*, *51*(3), 263–274. DOI: https://10.1002/jocb.123

Storme, M., Myszkowski, N., Baron, S., et al. (2019). Same test, better scores: Boosting the reliability of short online intelligence recruitment tests with nested logit item response theory models. *Journal of Intelligence, 7*(3), 1–17. DOI: https://10.3390/jintelligence7030017

Storme, M., Myszkowski, N., Çelik, P., et al. (2014). Learning to judge creativity: The underlying mechanisms in creativity training for non-expert judges. *Learning and Individual Differences, 32*, 19–25. DOI: https://10.1016/j.lindif.2014.03.002

Stout, W., Habing, B., Douglas, J., et al. (1996). Conditional covariance-based nonparametric multidimensionality assessment. *Applied Psychological Measurement, 20*(4), 331–354. DOI: https://10.1177/014662169602000403

Suh, Y., & Bolt, D. M. (2010). Nested logit models for multiple-choice item response data. *Psychometrika, 75*(3), 454–473. DOI: https://10.1007/s11336-010-9163-7

Tan, M., Mourgues, C., Hein, S., et al. (2015). Differences in judgments of creativity: How do academic domain, personality, and self-reported creativity influence novice judges' evaluations of creative productions? *Journal of Intelligence, 3*(3), 73–90. DOI: https://10.3390/jintelligence3030073

Thissen, D. (2001). Psychometric engineering as art. *Psychometrika, 66*(4), 473–485. DOI: https://10.1007/BF02296190

Thissen, D., & Steinberg, L. (1986). A taxonomy of item response models. *Psychometrika, 51*(4), 567–577. DOI: https://10.1007/BF02295596

Thissen, D., Steinberg, L., & Gerrard, M. (1986). Beyond group-mean differences: The concept of item bias. *Psychological Bulletin, 99*(1), 118–128. DOI: https://10.1037/0033-2909.99.1.118

van der Linden, W. J. (2005). *Linear models for optimal test design.* New York: Springer-Verlag.

van der Linden, W. J. (2006). A lognormal model for response times on test items. *Journal of Educational and Behavioral Statistics, 31*(2), 181–204. DOI: https://10.3102/10769986031002181

van der Linden, W. J. (2016). Introduction. In *Handbook of item response theory, Volume 1: Models* (1 ed.), (pp. 1–10). Boca Raton, FL: CRC Press. DOI: https://10.1201/9781315374512

van der Linden, W. J., Klein Entink, R. H., & Fox, J.- P. (2010). IRT parameter estimation with response times as collateral information. *Applied Psychological Measurement, 34*(5), 327–347. DOI: https://10.1177/0146621609349800

van der Maas, H. L. J., Dolan, C. V., Grasman, R. P. P. P., et al. (2006). A dynamical model of general intelligence: The positive manifold of intelligence by mutualism. *Psychological Review, 113*(4), 842–861. DOI: https://10.1037/0033-295X.113.4.842

van Duijn, M. A. J., & Jansen, M. G. H. (1995). Modeling repeated count data: Some extensions of the Rasch Poisson counts model. *Journal of Educational and Behavioral Statistics, 20*(3), 241. DOI: https://10.2307/1165402

Wagenmakers, E.- J., & Farrell, S. (2004). AIC model selection using Akaike weights. *Psychonomic Bulletin & Review, 11*(1), 192–196. DOI: https://10.3758/BF03206482

Weiss, D. J. (1982). Improving measurement quality and efficiency with adaptive testing. *Applied Psychological Measurement, 6*(4), 473–492. DOI: https://10.1177/014662168200600408

Yen, W. M. (1981). Using simulation results to choose a latent trait model. *Applied Psychological Measurement, 5*(2), 245–262. DOI: https://10.1177/014662168100500212

Zinbarg, R. E., Yovel, I., Revelle, W., et al. (2006). Estimating generalizability to a latent variable common to all of a scale's indicators: A comparison of estimators for ω_h. *Applied Psychological Measurement, 30*(2), 121–144. DOI: https://10.1177/0146621605278814

Cambridge Elements ≡

Creativity and Imagination

Anna Abraham
University of Georgia, USA

Anna Abraham, Ph.D. is the E. Paul Torrance Professor at the University of Georgia, USA. Her notable publications include *The Neuroscience of Creativity* (2018, Cambridge University Press) and the edited volume, *The Cambridge Handbook of the Imagination* (2020).

About the Series

Cambridge Elements in Creativity and Imagination publishes original perspectives and insightful reviews of empirical research, methods, theories, or applications in the vast fields of creativity and the imagination. The series is particularly focused on showcasing novel, necessary and neglected perspectives.

Cambridge Elements ⁼

Creativity and Imagination

Elements in the Series

Printed in the United States
by Baker & Taylor Publisher Services